Don't [illegible].

CW01636837

A memoir uncovering the hidden difficulties of dyslexia.

JO REES

Copyright © 2017 Jo Rees
Illustrations by Mark O'Brien

All rights reserved.

Ed. 2
ISBN-13: 978-1-9998008-1-9

DEDICATION

To those I did not know, but who smiled at me.
To those whose unconditional love continues to protect me.
This is what I have achieved because of you.

CONTENTS

WINTER

SPRING

ACKNOWLEDGMENTS

My Mum and Dad, because they made me who I am.

My 'Trumpet Playing Husband', who has been nothing but patient over the last few years, has made me endless cups of tea and who did not let me give up.

My children who have spent hours occupying themselves while I wrote, edited, and worked with people on the book.

My family and friends, who continue to support me no matter what.

To all the teachers who took the time to smile at me and nurtured me through some of the hardest years of my life.

The pupils, and their families, who I work with and support. They continue to inspire me and remind me what life is really about.

Lois who set me free.

'Unbiological' for being my 'revolution', and encouraging me to write this in the first place.

David Rees for his words of encouragement, advice, and support in developing the structure of the book.

Tricia, for believing in me when I did not.

Yvonne and Bernadette for providing the final push.

'Always There' who read every word and line at least 3 times to make sure it was 'just' right.

Mark O'Brien for being more dyslexic than me, and for tolerating hours of me reading sections of the book out to him as he created the most poignant of illustrations that feature throughout.

My sister for putting up with a high-maintenance sister her whole life, and designing the cover!

'Windsay' for fine tuning the cover, and for their perfectionist touches!

And finally, Mr. 'Always There'. Without him there would be no 'actual' book. Without him, there would have 'just' been some A4 pages scattered with text, illustrations on scraps of paper, not to mention probably so many more typos, grammatical errors, and incorrect punctuation!

I will be forever indebted to you all.

XXXXX

"To be defined is not to dwell on what you cannot do, but to expose, polish and shine the things you choose to do.

Only when you have exposed, polished and shined your strengths, are you able to be all that you are meant to be.

This is my definition, and this is my expectation of you."

(Jo Rees, 2015)

A LETTER TO THE READER

When I started writing this book it was with a view to creating something that would support my son and godson in understanding their dyslexia to get them through a difficult patch. As I started to write, the words just poured out of me in a way that felt right and eased my soul and so my story was etched on a page, somehow more real and more poignant than it had ever been. As close friends read it, I discovered that despite believing all my life that my written word was inadequate, I possessed a skill of putting words together to make memories dance and come to life once more. As more people read it, I was told the way I put words together was so powerful I could move strangers to tears and teach people I knew something they didn't know about me, but more importantly something that they didn't know about dyslexia.

My dyslexia had been hidden behind my dazzling smile; I was accomplished at hiding it, but I learnt through revisiting my past that it had only hindered my progress in life. Whilst writing my story it wasn't always easy to delve back into the past and know which parts to include and which parts to leave out. Whilst on most occasions the honesty felt necessary to be able to get people to understand the anguish and internal battles people with dyslexia face, it left me vulnerable and exposed. As more people read it I began to realise that unintentionally the narrative I had forged was dark and raw in places, creating images of a broken person living in a virtual prison, limping through life. This had never been my intention but had been my internal reality for so long I had not realised, because it was the only way I knew to live.

It is not all dark; light shone regularly into my world in the shape of my family and close friends. I harnessed it, stored it internally, and used it as hope and resilience to get me through my life. It gave me the courage to keep going, keep battling, but most importantly to keep achieving and moving forward positively through my life. The honesty is not designed to shock you or pull you into a dark place with me, but to show you where the darkness is within dyslexia and where it can hide, so that you know where to look and what to watch for.

By writing this book I have set myself free. I have shared my story because I want to make a difference to the world, to develop awareness and understanding of dyslexia, and to change the wider perception of the ways in which dyslexia can manifest itself. I hope the way the words are put together and the memories I have shared will enable you to experience standing in my shoes, so that it changes the way you view dyslexia for the better.

I feel that dyslexia is often misunderstood by educational professionals within schools. It is a 'buzzword' schools flippantly use. Often teachers are aware of the diagnosis but don't really understand or know what to do about it. I hear and witness it often:

'Oh yes, that child is dyslexic'

'Spelling and reading are slow'

'She struggles to organise herself'

'He reverses his letters, and just can't get his ideas onto paper'

'He's an August baby and perhaps he is just not very bright!'

'He is lazy because he can tell me all about what

he has learnt but refuses to get it onto paper!'

I believe that what teachers are told, and are taught whilst training, only touches the surface, and provides only a bare bones theory of dyslexia. I think that the true difficulties a person with dyslexia experiences are hidden, simply because we as dyslexics do all we can to hide them. We are clever and intelligent, experts at developing strategies to cope and we don't want to let people down. It's not that we cannot learn, we simply need to learn differently.

I wanted to tell you how understanding dyslexia comes not only from understanding the theory. It is far more than a diagnosis, it is far more than additional reading practise, handwriting practise and extra phonics. I wanted to show you how it leaks into everything we do, how it spills into every hour of every day, and how we can never get away from it. I want to make people realise how everyday normal events and comments, including those that most people could simply brush off, can have a profound effect on how a dyslexic can view themselves, and how this goes on to affect their daily life. This can ultimately stop them from fulfilling their potential and perhaps lead to difficulties with mental health.

What if a person with dyslexia has, deep within themselves, the ability to find a cure for cancer, or has the ability to find alternative energy sources or can solve world hunger? We may never know if schools continue to teach with a 2D approach. Education needs to learn to look under the surface, to look beyond a label and beyond the theory; to look at the person beneath. This is the only thing I wish I could change in my past. I wish my teachers had taken the time to look beneath my smile, because that would have made a world of difference to me.

Intelligence:

"The ability to acquire knowledge, develop skills and think for one's self to solve problems."

(Jo Rees, 2017)

PROLOGUE: CONFESSION

My name is Jo Rees, and I am thirty-six years old.

I can't usually write a cheque accurately the first time.

I can't read train, boat or bus timetables accurately.

I can't text and talk.

I can't spell words with more than three syllables, or words with complicated vowel patterns.

I don't know my times tables by heart.

I have lost more keys than I have had locks for.

Despite writing lots of lists I always forget something, usually the thing I need most!

I can't remember more than two verbal instructions and don't think in a straight line.

I miss appointments all the time; not intentionally, I just forget, double book myself, and end up feeling stupid.

I have only completely read ten fiction books since I was thirteen - three of these are the 50 Shades of Grey trilogy and the other seven are Harry Potter.

I still have to think really hard to work out the difference between a noun, a verb, and an adjective.

I can't understand what I am reading unless I read it at least five times.

I did not know my left from my right until I was twenty-three.

I have never got an A grade for a written exam.

I cannot proofread my own work.

I always feel out of my depth.

I always feel like an underdog.

I rarely feel confident on the inside.

I thought I was unintelligent, hadn't worked hard

enough, and needed to try harder… that was until I trained to become a specialist teacher of dyslexia.

It turned out that I am, in fact, dyslexic; however, I had been dyslexic for thirty-four years before I discovered it…

But here's the revelation: I am really intelligent, incredibly resilient, brave, and pretty amazing to have achieved all that I have. Against all the odds I have achieved…

10 GCSEs

3 A-levels

A 2:1 Degree in Dance, Drama and English in Contemporary Culture

3 Postgraduate Certificates

Nurture group network accreditation

1 Diploma in Dyslexia and Literacy

Specialist Teacher status,

… and all of this without one minute of extra time

offered!

I lived, blissfully unaware, with undiagnosed dyslexia until I was studying for my Postgraduate Certificate and Diploma in Dyslexia when I was twenty-eight. It was while studying for this that I realised I probably was dyslexic, however, I only finally plucked up enough courage to get it diagnosed when I was thirty-four.

I **know** what it is like to live with dyslexia.

I **know** how exhausting it is to stay one step ahead of the game in constant fear of falling behind, knowing if I fall behind I'll never catch up.

I **know** the feeling of dread when being handed the pen to scribe whilst working in a group, knowing that I won't even be able to spell the simplest of words, all with the feeling that everyone is watching me.

I **know** how dyslexics battle to stay on top of life's organisation; remembering appointments, remembering what you need from the shop, all whilst thinking ahead for the next few days.

I **know** how dyslexics battle daily to hide how bad they feel about themselves, not understanding why they feel that they cannot do the simplest of things, despite giving 110%.

I **know** how no one **EVER** notices that a person with dyslexia is giving 110% and how much this pains and hurts them inside.

I know all these things because **this is my life too**.

I **know** through my teaching experience and specialist learning the best ways to identify and teach a dyslexic learner, so that they can thrive and achieve their potential, going on to become confident learners with the knowledge that anything is possible. I have empowered many of the children I have taught to understand that they can be anything they want to be, reading and writing ability does not define them. Reading and writing is only a small part of what we need to be successful. Just because a pupil has struggled to learn to read and write, does not mean that they cannot be exactly what they wish to be; a doctor, a policeman, a business woman, a newspaper reporter, a bank manager or even a politician!

I **know** what it is like to be the parent of a dyslexic child. I have had and continue to have the battles with my son over reading every night, completing homework, practising spellings, and practising multiplication tables.

I **know** what it is like to watch your child hurt because they feel they are rubbish at everything, because they can't read at the same speed as the rest of their class.

I **know** how much it hurts as a parent to not be able to control how your child feels about themselves; how your child can't see the things that are wonderful about them, because all your child can see is what they can't do; because they have to go to school every day and, once there, their ability to read and write is continually measured, recorded and compared against benchmarks.

I **know** how much you love the school holidays because you know that the hideous relentless battles about school won't be there for a few weeks.

I **know** how much you dread the younger sibling making progress because the gap is closing in on your older dyslexic child.

I **know** how this can instil panic within, leaving a feeling of being divided and uneasy, because I too am in this place every day.

If you are dyslexic, I hope that this book shows

you ways to overcome the difficulties you face in everyday life and how you must never give up on your dreams. I want you to know that if you have feelings of inadequacy, low confidence, and low self-esteem you are not alone. I want you to know that there is hope and that if life feels hard right now, with the right support and a pinch of self-belief anything is possible.

SUMMER

Hope:

"To believe that what is wished for can come true."

(Jo Rees, 2017)

DIAGNOSIS

I approach the enormous front door with a confident unease. I stop. I stand on the doorstep and take a few deep breaths. The air is sticky and smells of summer. The July sun still hangs high in the sky, exposed and vulnerable against the unclouded blue. It is 7pm but the rays still shine down, bouncing off the leaves on the nearby trees, reflecting on anything which is in their way, and accentuating the hidden beauties of the inevitably arriving dusk.

Do I really want to know? After thirty-four years, is it really that important to know? What if I am not dyslexic? Would that just make me stupid and maybe unintelligent?

I take another deep breath. A breath that tries to settle the flutters of anticipation in my tummy. Excitement or fear, I just can't tell. I raise my hand and knock purposefully on the door in front of me.

A few seconds later, the door opens and I am greeted by a respected colleague. All I can see is her smile. A smile that radiates warmth and puts me at ease; a smile that says you can trust me, you're safe and we will do this together. Immediately, I feel the butterflies shift; they shift towards excited anticipation.

We sit in the kitchen making small talk, whilst my colleague makes us tea. We avoid eye contact with each other. She feels as uncomfortable as I do. I am one of the leading SENDCos (Special Educational Needs and disability Co-ordinator) in my area. I have a reputation for being confident and delivering work of a good standard. I have twelve years' experience in primary teaching. I ran one of four specialist provisions for dyslexic pupils at the age of twenty-seven. I work hard and I don't let people down. I am an advocate for pupils and parents of pupils with SEND.

I don't see any of this. I don't feel any of this. I feel like a fake and I feel like I am not good enough, equal or important. I feel deep down I am a fraud and I am preparing for the lady known as 'The Smile' to discover this.

After a few minutes of making awkward small talk, I begin to justify my reasons for thinking I am dyslexic out loud. 'The Smile' looks at me with gentle kindness and admiration, I think. She tells me I am brave. She asks me if I am ready to start.

As we begin the cognitive assessments, I know I am going to find this hard. Not necessarily because I think I am unintelligent, but because I know these tests are going to expose something I have worked my whole life to hide.

Veiling my vulnerability, sheer terror and excitement behind my fixed smile, we begin with a non-verbal test. I am handed cubes with shapes on them: black and yellow triangles or squares. I am shown a picture. My task is to use the cubes to recreate the picture in front of me. Initially, I start well. I manipulate the pieces easily and recreate the shape.

Quite quickly the pictures I must recreate become more challenging, but then the real challenge begins. It has nothing to do with cubes and shapes, but I can feel it starting in my stomach. My anxiety is rising. I swallow it down. It is like bile, it burns and it tastes foul, but I can cope with it. I can keep it hidden and I can control it.

Despite the fading sun and the chill seeping into the mid-evening air, I start to sweat. I can feel my heart pounding and my brain starting to fog. My smile widens, but I can't think straight. I am becoming less logical and less efficient at handling and moving the pieces.

Next, we approach a task where I am shown a row of pictures with one missing. I am instructed to view another row of pictures and select the correct one to complete the first row. My anxiety is cranking up now. I am hot and sweaty with a racing pulse. The burning is rising from my stomach up into my chest, but still I continue to keep a lid on it. No one needs to know the lid is there. After years of controlling the burning, this is second nature to me. Instinct. Fight or flight. I always pick fight, but no one knows. My body keeps me protected and safe. Outwardly, I remain positive. I smile and I do my best. Some of the pictures are more like complex diagrams and make no sense to me.

As we approach the verbal test, the one I am secretly really dreading, I can feel cracks forming on the virtual lid. 'The Smile' says a word and I must explain what the word means. This is tricky. I can't seem to put my thoughts into sentences. I can only think of single words. Word association and hoping for the best is the strategy I employ to get me through this task. This and a lot of guess work! The anxiety that the guess work provokes ups the ante and adds another dimension to the game. It's creeping, bubbling, lifting the lid; I am conscious and aware of this feeling all the time. No time to relax or become complacent. Part of my mind is on controlling my body language and reactions. I will not let this beat me. I will see this through.

I approach the reading comprehension task. I am given a paragraph of text to read. A sea of letters that make words and sentences. I am then asked questions and timed whilst reading it. At this point I have arrived at a destination in my mind. I am firmly stranded in a desert of no hope; a dot on the landscape. I am held captive here, but no one is holding me hostage. I have placed myself here, chosen this of my own free will. On the surface, all

'The 'Smile' sees is me reflecting her smile back at her, a smile which portrays calm and confidence. Behind my smiley demeanour more cracks are forming.

I know I won't have time to read the whole text so I skim read it, looking for key words. The only problem is all the words look like key words, so this strategy is not really working. I follow the text with my finger and read quickly in my head. I realise I don't understand what I'm reading, all I am doing is decoding the letters. Time runs out. I am asked questions and I am mostly making guesses. This strategy works well initially and I scrape through the first three or four paragraphs. By paragraph five this strategy is useless.

The paragraphs are getting longer and more involved. 'It is okay' I tell myself, I have more strategies I can draw on. For my next strategy, I read as much as I can in the time that I have, but I read it thoroughly and hope that I will understand it. I won't be able to read it all but maybe the question will be about the bit I have read.

The evening darkness is creeping into the room and choking my smile. In my head, I chant my mantra of thirty plus years, 'keep trying, keep listening, keep working hard, keep battling on.' I keep providing answers, I am mostly guessing, but it seems to be enough to get by. Gradually and inevitably the words become more and more blurred, and I am able to make less and less sense of them. I keep going. I keep fighting and battling, but eventually I admit defeat and answer a question with.

'I don't know.'

The lid is off; the anxiety has overwhelmed my thoughts and my ability to think rationally. The darkness has won, night has fallen and I am alone with no way out. My judgement is totally clouded by the mist of insecurities that flood through my body like an icy tidal wave.

It physically pains me to answer a question with 'I don't know', when the information I need is right in front of me and I have been given the time to read it. It hurts. I feel that I should be able to answer the question. I should have read it quicker and then I could have made more sense of it, if only I were concentrating harder. These feelings of hurt and uselessness resonate through my body, filling every millimetre, finally settling and attaching themselves to existing cracks and crevices, gouging them deeper and confirming that they are there.

These crevices have been created by years of feeling stupid, unintelligent and out of my depth. It is the most excruciating kind of hurt I have ever experienced, because I'm doing it to myself. I have actively placed myself in a position where I know I'm out of my depth, but I secretly hoped and wished and dreamed that maybe this time it would be different. Maybe this time the penny would drop and maybe this would be the time I finally understood, because I had concentrated hard enough.

We begin the spelling test. I have not given up but my weaknesses are out there and she knows. 'The Smile' can see it. She sees right through me now. I am exposed and transparent. Vulnerable. I pick up the pencil, resigning myself to the fact that there is no longer a place to hide. The darkness surrounds me and my only way out is to trust and follow 'The Smile'. I know that my best will not be enough to score a good mark, because I cannot spell. I cannot find the right letters for the sounds, and I cannot get the letters in the right order.

Despite this, I approach the test confidently but within a few moments the words become too challenging for me to write accurately. I don't give up, but I know that my attempts will be laughable. I only keep going because as 'The Smile' provides each word I need to spell she gives me a knowing, trusting smile that tells me I am safe and I am ok. She will not judge me. This is what enables me to keep going and to manage the feelings of inadequacy, worthlessness and unimportance that seep out of me with every failed word I write.

I feel sure that 'The Smile' will not allow the results of this test to define her expectations and thoughts of me. 'The Smile' will still value my input at meetings and ask for my opinion. To her, regardless of the outcome, I'll still be the same person who walked through her door four hours ago.

My exterior smiles and laughs through this spelling test. I know it is pointless covering it up, but after years of having a default setting it is what I'm programmed to do. Smile. Smile as if your life depended on it, because often my life did depend on it. I continue, but now verbalise my thoughts: 'I am hopeless at spelling' and 'I will give it a try'. This helps justify my choices as I combine letters, knowing that they are incorrect and ridiculous, but hoping that she will be able to read them.

The assessment is nearing its end, but there are still diagnostic memory tests to go, auditory and visual ones. There is nowhere left to hide. There are no lifelines, just 'The Smile'. I pull out my secret weapons, determination and resilience. I have learnt to never give up. In the cool darkness, I continue by putting one foot in front of another knowing a miracle will happen, because miracles do happen if you just believe and I know that this is not over yet. I have reached a point where I am thinking: What is the worst that can happen? With brave disregard, I provide responses to the questions, not knowing if I am saying what she needs to hear, but at the same time not really caring anymore. As she writes down my responses in black biro, she has seen my Achilles heel; it is there in black and white in front of her.

After hours of assessments, we are done. 'The Smile' makes more tea. We are still in the brightly lit room, while the night sky stares at us through the window. The tea sits steaming on the table as I sit, uncomfortably surrounded by harsh electric light, wondering for one final time what the results will be. The minutes drag and feel like hours but finally 'The Smile' has finished scoring and is intrigued by the results. I am not. They confirm everything I suspected. The cognitive assessments see scores in the middle of average range. I have a slight strength in non-verbal ability, but it is not significant and is indicative of a typical dyslexic profile.

I explained when I arrived that I have to read things many times to understand them, and the reading comprehension score confirms this. The result indicates reading comprehension on a first read is in the below average range.

I'm not upset. Strangely I feel relieved that I am not going mad. I did not waste all that time at university reading and re-reading texts in my room. An unknown feeling echoes faintly through my mind; this is what it feels like to be proud. I am not super intelligent; my reading score is low but despite this I do fine. It has not stopped me. Perhaps I am clever to have developed strategies to overcome this significant difficulty in comprehending texts.

The spelling result is lower than low, but this does not quieten the whispers of feeling good which are growing louder in my head! Surprisingly, I don't actually care about this score. I've coped this far as a poor speller and will continue to cope in any way I can. The only difference is I feel I can worry even less about it now, because I know it is a genuine difficulty, and that my brain is responsible, not me.

I await the auditory working memory score thinking nothing can hurt me now. I feel invincible. 'The Smile' announces my score: 5th percentile. Out of one hundred people my age, ninety-five would perform better than me. 'The Smile' tells me my auditory working memory is, in fact, worse than this because I employed so many strategies during these tests. She tells me I closed my eyes, I whispered the numbers under my breath to help remember them, I was counting the numbers on my fingers. I had no idea I was using these strategies because to me they are second nature and what I have learnt to use to get by. Evolution. Survival. I knew no different. I thought it was what everybody did.

What I had long suspected had been confirmed. I am dyslexic. I sit opposite 'The Smile' quietly taking it all in. After thirty-four years of believing it was my fault, that if I just worked harder maybe I could do better, I was living proof that intelligence and learning profiles are only part of the story. With ability results in the middle of average and a severe diagnosis of dyslexia, I had achieved GCSEs, A-levels, a degree, PGCEs and a Postgraduate Diploma, all without one minute of extra time or support.

I sit awkwardly at the table feeling like I am under the spotlight, because outside darkness has properly fallen. Night time has arrived and has to be survived, before the sun will rise once again. I wonder if I should cry, but instead I choose to laugh out loud. 'The Smile' laughs with me. The laughter overwhelms me, washing relief through me, filling and cleansing the crevices in my soul in preparation to start letting them heal. I feel phenomenal. It is not me. I am not stupid. I am not unintelligent. I am just dyslexic.

I have limped my way through life so far, always working incredibly hard. I can see this now, having never seen it or been prepared to acknowledge it before, but right now it is all I can see.

As I step back through the enormous door, into the darkness and fresh air, the moonlight shines on our faces. She still smiles at me and it is not a smile of pity like I feared it could be. It is a smile of adulation.

I know she watched me as I walked to the end of the drive, but I did not look back. I will never look back. I am strong, I am brave and I have found the answers I need that will allow me to find my true self and live a fulfilled life every day.

My thoughts and feelings immediately shifted from myself, because this discovery was not about me, it was never about me. This was about needing proof that I had overcome dyslexia. This meant that there was hope for all the pupils I worked with and that there was hope for my dyslexic son.

At this time, I had no idea that three years later my world would completely fall apart, and from a place of desperation and darkness, I would find the strength and courage to make a difference to other lives by writing it all down in a book.

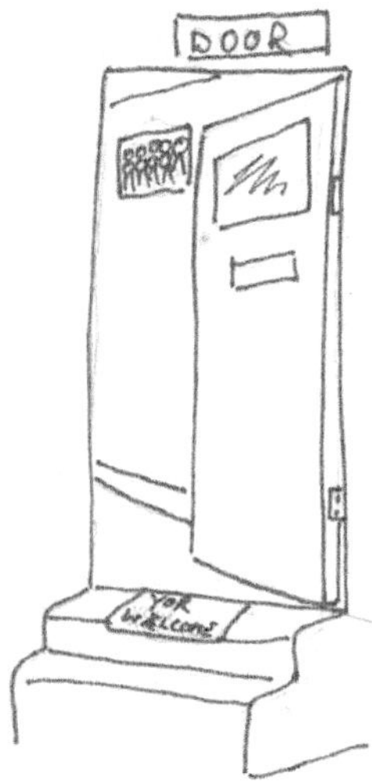
DOOR
YOR
WELCOME

CHILDHOOD

The early years of childhood felt like endless summer. I grew up in an end of terrace three-bedroom house, in a cul-de-sac, with my mum, my dad and my younger sister. We went to the local schools, we did our homework and we played outside with the other children in our street. We were a typical working-class family. Dad worked nights in a factory that manufactured parts for aircraft. He was one of hundreds of men who did the physical labour required to machine and rivet the parts. Dad rarely read me stories or helped with homework. Mum did that. Dad had left school with nothing other than a cycling proficiency badge, but he was great at solving practical problems. Dad built amazing things from wood: desks, bookshelves and toolboxes.

My Mum didn't work when we were little, and I can remember glorious summers spent on the beach with my younger cousins, auntie and uncle. Every year we had a joint family holiday to Devon for a week, travelling together in a minibus. It always involved playing cards, rounders, scampi and chips and homemade cake!

I know I loved school and at the age of four, I could not wait to go. I was keen to learn to read and write. I remember I bought home small cards which had hand written words on in a tobacco tin, which I read through every night with my mum at my request. I had these cards alongside books called *Roger Red Hat* and *Billy Blue Hat*, who were friends with Johnny and Jennifer Yellow Hat. They lived in the Village with Three Corners. I remember I learnt to read quickly, flying through book after book, and tin after tin of words.

I read and I read. In those days, we didn't have reading records and progress wasn't measured in anywhere near the depth it is today. By the end of year 3, I was considered a free reader and read Enid Blyton books like they were going out of fashion. *Famous Five*, *Secret Seven* and *Naughty Amelia Jane.* A book every few days. No one knew I was not really understanding what I was reading. No one checked.

My spelling was atrocious; my mum was concerned and asked my teachers on several occasions if this would ever be looked at. She was constantly told, 'Jo has so many ideas, it's important that she gets them onto paper and the spelling will come later.'

It was at the age of eight, in the October of 1987, as the leaves drifted from the trees and autumn set in, that a real-life tragedy happened to my family. I lost both of my grandads, three months apart; this was my first experience of death, loss and grief.

I remember my grandads vividly – as the first grandchild on both sides of the family, I saw them once or twice a week, and had a secure attachment to both of them. My dad's dad in particular, who had always been seen as the impatient, intolerant, and grumpy old man, turned to mush when he saw me. I sat on his lap, we sang songs, we played games. He taught me the colours of the rainbow - **R**ichard **O**f **Y**ork **G**ave **B**attle **I**n **V**ain. My mum's dad taught me how to play cards; they both showed me unconditional love and compassion.

My mum's dad died first, in October, twelve days before my birthday. The result of years of working with asbestos-lagged pipes as a naval plumber, saw his life end with lung cancer. Dad's dad died three months later of a heart attack from being overweight, drinking and smoking too much and having a hugely stressful job. He was a self-made man, an entrepreneur having built his own company from nothing.

When they died, the world stopped and shifted direction. I don't remember the sun shining anymore, I can rarely remember laughing. At the age of only eight, I felt that my childhood had ended. I felt empty. I constantly had tummy ache and cried all the time.

Despite this grief my parents kept everything as normal as they could for me and my sister, and where possible continued as if nothing had happened. This was the biggest issue for me. It had happened, and I wish that they had spent more time acknowledging that it had happened. This may have made it easier for me to deal with. This however was my parents' way of trying to protect us and keep us safe from further hurt.

In addition, my teachers at primary school didn't really understand the grief I was carrying and didn't push me academically either. My male teacher got frustrated with me when I cried ALL the time. I knew I was disappointing him, but I had nothing left to give to anyone else. I was trying to carry on but it was so hard. I only had six months left until I had to move to middle school.

Winter came and went and spring arrived. At the age of nine, I knew that I didn't want to place any more stress on my mum and dad. I felt that my role was just to get on with life and keep my head down, trying not to make it any more difficult for my parents than it already was.

Grief makes you grow up quickly. In public I could cope, but when I was at home, I wanted to be alone and to feel sad. This caused huge arguments between me and my younger sister, not only at this point, but throughout our lives. It seemed that she hadn't been affected by what had happened. She appeared to be carrying on like normal, and this made me angry. This was wrong of me, as she must have been affected, but I was experiencing grief for the first time and I didn't understand the range of emotions that come with it. I know now that anger is an emotion inherently embedded in the grieving process, and looking back I was angry at the world, not at her.

Grief made me sensible, it made me play safe, it made me want to be invisible. I know I drove my sister mad when I refused to make the den that would make mess for mum and dad to clear up, or to stay out late when we were older, but I was coming from a place of pain, a place of wanting to support mum and dad, a place of not really wanting to exist in the real world. My confidence had dwindled and I felt like I was nothing to anyone in particular. If my grandads were not there to smile, then there really was no point in smiling at all unless you really had to.

The death of my grandads shaped my perception of myself. I felt I had failed, but I couldn't verbalise this to anyone. Inside I was broken, but outside I painted on a smile and hoped that tomorrow I would feel better. At the age of nine, I had started to employ strategies to keep my true feelings hidden from everyone - a dangerous game to play.

SCHOOL

Soon after losing my grandads, I hit middle school, supposedly a very good reader who was gifted at English. Transitions between schools are vulnerable times for all pupils, especially pupils with additional needs or risk factors, such as parental separation or grief. Whilst I mostly hated school by now, no one knew, because I smiled and I tried and I worked hard.

During this time, I stumbled across some amazing teachers who nurtured me through - Mr and Mrs E., and Miss S. mostly. They always seemed to be in the right place at the right time, with a genuine smile for me on their faces. They were like the shoots in spring pushing through the hard ground. Frosts can't keep them down, and if you wait long enough they will inevitably appear. Those teachers didn't give up on me and made my days lighter and more bearable.

It was here at middle school, that I discovered through constant berating that 'are', 'our,' and 'hour' are, in fact, three completely different words. They all sounded the same to me. I also discovered that there is no 'r' in 'warter', although this still makes no sense to me, as I can hear one if I say it aloud in my Isle of Wight accent!

I suddenly hated reading, and did it less and less because it took me so long and I never understood the stories properly. Despite this, I worked hard and the teachers loved me. The teachers loved me, but my peers did not. I was bullied badly at middle school, repeatedly called a swot, constantly picked on because I worked hard and was also perceived as being really clever. The devastating truth was that I was exhausted, broken inside and desperate for someone to notice the real me. The difficulty was, no one really knew who 'me' was as I was doing such a great job of hiding how I was really feeling. It is also really difficult for people to like you, when you don't like yourself.

Miss S. was my guardian angel at middle school. She just 'got me.' She saw my talent for acting and singing, she scooped me into the school choir and rescued me most lunchtimes by asking me to come and rehearse for this song or that song.

I became lonely and isolated, but still smiled on the outside and still completed my work. I fell off the top spot I had held at primary school and did not really understand why, because I was working so hard and doing everything my teachers asked of me. However, increasingly I never felt good enough and never seemed to be organised or on top of what was happening.

I had become the queen of 'blagging.' I got exceptionally good at pretending to read. None of the teachers ever noticed. I managed to keep up with class readers somehow; it was refreshing to be read to, to hear the words pour out in a fluent, exciting and expressive manner read by the class teacher. These shared reading sessions showed me that books could be interesting and full of escapism and knowledge.

I decided at middle school that I wanted to learn to play an instrument. My mum encouraged me. I picked the clarinet. My clarinet teacher did not really take to me! This was not her fault; I'm sure I was an infuriating student! I didn't mean to be, I just didn't seem to be able to help it. I couldn't make sense of the musical notes; I couldn't read them quickly enough; I struggled to follow all the auditory instructions and often became overwhelmed and just couldn't keep up.

The clarinet teacher seemed to have little patience with me. I know I was a hindrance in her lessons, because I couldn't keep up with the others in the group. This was not helping my confidence or making me feel good about myself. I battled on and managed to do my Grade One exam. I can remember being an absolute mess as I entered the room. I know I made loads of errors but, somehow, I scraped a pass.

After this exam, I gave up the clarinet. I don't generally give up; it's not in my makeup. However, I think that there is something to be said for knowing when you are fighting a battle that cannot be won without a significant amount of hard work, or one that only results in damaging yourself. By giving up, I was protecting myself from further failure and from having my confidence knocked further. I didn't have to learn an instrument at this time. This was not a priority. I was struggling with the basics: reading, writing, maths and social skills. These were causing me enough stress. Subconsciously, I decided to focus on the essentials.

Meanwhile, my evenings were filled with dancing and singing. I took tap, modern and ballet classes. I was good at this and went most nights. On the nights I didn't have a class, I danced in my bedroom. Listening to my tapes of musicals, I knew the words to nearly all of them by heart: Me and My Girl, Anything Goes, Singing in the Rain, Cats and Les Misérables. Both in these classes and in my bedroom, it felt like an endless summer. I could pretend I was someone; I could pretend I mattered, I could be special, I could be me. I didn't need anyone else to be happy. I danced until it hurt and sung until I was empty.

This was escapism at its extreme. I knew all the words. I learnt them by osmosis and by listening again and again. Not once did I read the words. I just learnt them. Lyrics to thousands and thousands of musicals and 90s hits. Music makes me genuinely smile and got me through my teenage years. For a few hours every day, I was free; free of pretending, free of stress, free from feeling like I was a stupid nothing. However, I would eventually have to return to the real world.

I soon became accomplished at turning on a smile and looking intelligent, even if I didn't feel intelligent. I was particularly good at talking, and I don't just mean chatting, although I'm quite good at this too! One of my special gifts is to be able to talk confidently and interestingly about things I am knowledgeable about.

In Year 7, at the age of eleven, we did a huge project in partnership with the Council on road safety and traffic calming, which directly affected our school site. The school won several prestigious awards and I was selected to represent the school at ceremonies in London. I did try to volunteer someone else for the second ceremony, because my selection was not helping my 'swot' status. However, it was decided by the teachers that I must go because of my presentation skills.

As a spin-off to these awards, we were recorded for local newspapers and local news programmes. I was selected to talk to the reporters for all of these things, withdrawn from lessons because I was thought of as making good progress academically. How could I not be when I was talking that confidently?

Years 7 and 8 went by in a blur of project work, representing the school and talking. Little reading or comprehension were required. Instead, I got by with opportunities for practical hands-on learning and a lot of blagging.

I didn't view my gift for talking as special. I viewed it as the thing that gave me the reputation of 'swot' and stopped me from having a normal school life. Perhaps if I had been in the classroom, I may have learnt more, who knows? But what I do know is my 'special gift' didn't really prepare me for high school, where things were about to reach a whole new level of difficulty for me.

HIGH SCHOOL

How I got through high school is still a mystery to me. I got up every day, bracing myself for the daily battle that would commence between myself, my brain and reality. I was working hard but struggling, and no one seemed to notice. My best never felt good enough.

I can remember sitting in GCSE English at the back of the class, trying to make myself as small as possible. Mr E. had told me I was good at English, but I found it increasingly difficult to understand. We studied Macbeth and I struggled to make sense of it. This was confusing to me as it was a play, and I loved plays and drama, so it should have been right up my street. Instead, it made me feel nervous, anxious and stupid.

The teacher used to read, and we had to follow. I couldn't keep up. She read too quickly. I used to trace my finger along the line, following the words, whilst inside my head I was shouting, increasingly more desperately, 'Stop! Please stop!'; 'I need to ask questions'; 'I need to re-read this'. Of course, she stopped eventually to quiz the class. I would slide down in my seat, hoping that she wouldn't notice me, while at the same time trying to go back to the beginning to read it again.

As she stopped asking questions, I was relieved; I had managed to escape this round of questioning, but how long could I keep this up for? I know I believed that I was not listening properly, or that I was missing something, or that I was not concentrating hard enough. All I was being asked to do was follow some text and listen and make comment on what I had read, but I didn't understand it.

I spent hours writing and studying, trying to make my Macbeth essays make sense. I hoped that maybe one day, I would get a B or maybe even a B+? Surely I must have been getting close to improving my marks? I read the study guides, watched the films. My essays seemed to drift off at tangents. I never knew what the teachers were looking for, so could never work out what I was missing.

The teachers in class didn't seem to be interested in helping me; they had their favourites and I was not one of them. They never came to my table and they never checked I understood. They were part of my game. I was hiding and they were letting me. I was the winner of all rounds of this imaginary game. They never seemed to be able to catch me out. I was the master of wearing an invisibility cloak.

I remember the relief as I left the classroom knowing I had managed to get through another lesson, without being noticed and without being asked a question; knowing I had won another virtual round of hide and seek. This quickly became my routine in all lessons, not just English; head down, work hard, go unnoticed, hope someone messed about and disrupted the lesson so it would be shorter.

I remember one day having a cover teacher for English, Mrs M. I still don't know why she picked me, but I remember she offered me the opportunity to work with her one lunchtime. At the point of her offering, I remember thinking I had lost this round of hide and seek, because she had noticed me. I went along to her classroom all the same. I remember showing her one of my essays and she simply said, 'your sentences are too long.' then paused. 'Let's work together to turn these long sentences into two or three shorter sentences. They will help you channel your thoughts.'

We worked solidly for twenty minutes. She smiled at me, encouraged me. She didn't ask me questions I could not answer, she improved my essay. I only remember having one session with Mrs M. and I know I got more inspiration and hope from this one session, than I had from any of my other English lessons.

The only time I could shine was in drama. The reason being, in drama you pretend to be someone else. I didn't need to be me. I could disappear and truly be invisible. I also loved my drama teacher Miss P. She became my lifeline at high school. Miss P. was a newly-qualified young teacher, enthusiastic, inspirational and most importantly good fun. Her lessons were enjoyable, but she pushed us hard, in a calculated, safe, and nurturing way. I did really well in drama practicals, getting A's most of the time. I lived for these sessions, to take part in the performances and learn more, all without opening a single book!

Art, with the lovely Miss S., was another lifeline,

but for a completely different reason. Art sessions were full of laughter, and I so needed to laugh. Miss S. was always smiling, and always embraced what we did, even if it was rubbish! For a few hours every week, my smile was genuine, and I was lifted from the eternal winter of loneliness I had created for myself. Miss S. provided constructive criticism that drove us forward and gave us feedback on how we could improve. She always commented on the smallest improvements and progress, she led by example and she showed me what to do.

Surprisingly, I was quite good at French. This is particularly ironic as my knowledge of the English language was so poor. I didn't know what a noun, verb, or adjective was! Learning French helped me get through English. I was able to ask questions about a new language that I felt unable to ask in the language I had been learning and using for fourteen years. I believe I did well, because the teacher, Mrs H., liked me. She seemed to have time for me and was patient. I felt that she believed in me.

I remember the smile that she gave me when I learnt something new, but also that the effort she put into me matched my own. More than anything, she noticed me. She also noticed I was losing weight and while I never seemed to be eating anything, she had noticed how hard I was working. I went to her three lunchtimes a week, and revisited what we had learnt in the previous lessons, slowly going over what I had misunderstood and unpicking what I didn't understand. The other refreshing thing about these sessions was that they involved no text at all. They were almost entirely verbal; aural sessions that used a white board on occasion, but on the whole, very little reading was required!

In science, I carefully positioned myself on the 'intelligent' table, sitting next to the super articulate and clever Charlotte. She clearly had no problems with her working memory! She was kind to me. She did not belittle me, but would instead explain, and re-explain, concepts I had not understood. She also allowed me to copy her notes when I hadn't been able to write them quickly enough.

I can only spell 'necessary' by reciting the rhyme that Charlotte taught to me in a science lesion: '**n**ever **e**at **c**hips **e**at **s**alad **s**andwiches **a**nd **r**emain **y**oung'. I have never forgotten it, and even today cannot spell the word without it. Charlotte is forever with me!

As my GCSEs loomed, my radiant smile hid a multitude of insecurities; low self-esteem and very little self-belief. I was beginning to feel helpless and desperate as I piled the pressure on myself not to reveal my feelings. I was losing weight, owing to the stress of the exams, and the fact I was desperately trying to be in control of something in a life that felt out of my control.

It did not take long to go from a size 12 to a size 8. I wanted to be smaller and smaller. However, alongside this addictive feeling, was an unexpected side effect. Feeling hungry meant I was feeling something. I often felt nothing, because I had made myself invisible. It reminded me I existed. This control over food only lasted for about six months. It was like everything in my life, I couldn't maintain it for long. The yo-yo dieting began. Over the next twenty years, I was not able to control what went into my mouth and gradually I just got bigger and bigger.

At fifteen I took an overdose of paracetamol. I'm still not sure to this day what I hoped to achieve. I didn't really want to die, but I didn't want to keep living like I was either. I needed help, but I wasn't sure what sort of help. Perhaps I just wanted to be noticed. I knew people saw me, but they didn't see the true me, because I used my dazzling smile as a shield to hide myself. Ironically, the wall I built to protect me kept everyone out, including my parents. My beautiful smile was becoming a grotesque weapon for self-destruction.

As well as losing weight, I had found another way to regulate my anxiety. When I felt I couldn't cope with the pressure or the stress of having to write an essay on something I didn't really understand, despite having read the book twice, attending all the lessons and completing all the homework, I would sit and scratch my cheek. When I say scratch, I really mean gouge my long nails into my beautiful, innocent flesh repeatedly, until I had blood under my fingernails. I can still remember the release. When I scratched, I felt something real. I felt euphoric. To feel something was better than to feel nothing, which is how I felt all the time.

It is not that my parents didn't notice this, because they did. However, once again I was the master of disguise. My face was already really dry owing to the hormones raging around my body and all the cream, facial wash and potions I was using to try and keep the acne at bay. This really helped me hide the marks on my face, as the skin just flaked away! I told my parents it was eczema, and that I scratched it in my sleep. I had never caused them any trouble, never lied to them, always been the good girl and just got on with it!

My mum, in particular, was really concerned and so we went to the GP who took one look, explaining that he really couldn't do anything to help. My mum was not happy with this and took matters into her own hands. She did some research, made some phone calls, and found an amazing skin doctor at the private hospital. She paid for an appointment and we went to see him. We went one Friday afternoon. He was a lovely smiley man, and he prescribed me some medication that would get rid of the acne, but would unfortunately have some side effects like dry skin, dry lips and loss of appetite.

I took the tablets, and over the next two years the acne slowly disappeared. However, I managed to get away with scratching my face and passing it off as eczema for the next two years. No-one ever questioned it. When it flared up, I just cut my nails short and donned the cotton gloves at night, appearing to all around me to be preventing the condition from getting any worse. However, the gloves would often come off in my sleep and I'd wake the following morning with blood on my hands, all the time with no-one knowing just how much I was dreading the thought of going to school.

HOBBIES

It makes me sad to think that my teachers never worked out what was going on, or stopped to look at me holistically. I was thriving in practical subjects and activities, but struggling in those involving reading and writing. Perhaps it is because I managed to retain a fake smile for most of the time, however, this was becoming more difficult to sustain. Even the things I was good at were becoming a struggle.

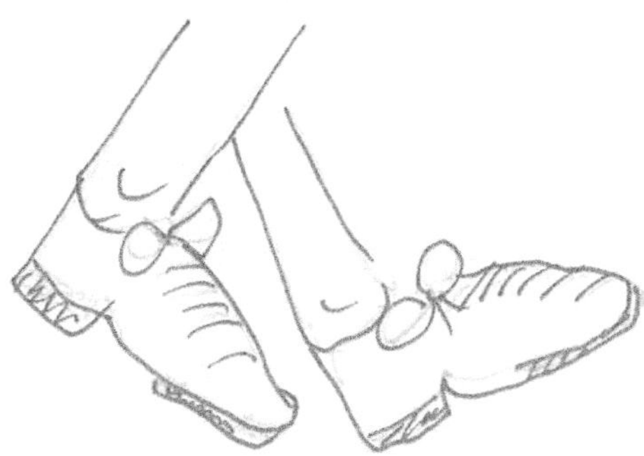

Out of school I loved to dance, and tap was my favourite. There was something magical about clicking your feet in time to music which soothed my soul. However, tap had picked up pace, and I just did not seem able to physically learn the steps quickly enough. Not understanding my needs or difficulties with processing, I just told myself 'must concentrate; must try harder.' Lesson after lesson, I watched girls pick up the steps on a first demonstration, while I had to ask again and again for them to be repeated, before practising for hours again once at home.

At fifteen I became the singer in a school band made up of five musicians, playing cover songs. The keyboard player could play nearly every instrument you gave him. There was also a sax player, trumpet player, drummer and pianist. They were the sensible and intelligent group in school. They won at awards evenings, and often represented the school. They were two years older than me. They had been asked to perform at an end of year concert and they asked me to sing with them. They wanted to do the Whitney Houston song 'One Moment in Time'. I felt about ten feet tall; I was younger than them, but they had chosen me to sing with them! I rehearsed with them a few times and sang the song repeatedly at home.

On the night, the theatre was full of students, parents and governors of the school, even the head teacher. I sang like I had never sung before. I sang with meaning and passion as if my life depended on it. It was one of the most amazing moments of my life, with the theatre breaking into spontaneous applause at the end. The smile on my face was real. I smiled naturally until my cheeks hurt.

After the evening had finished I can remember sitting in the emptying auditorium and looking at the stage. Suddenly, a man stood beside me. 'Wow, you have a voice!' he said. It was the headteacher. 'I'm really impressed.' He then walked away. Until this point, I'm not sure the headteacher even knew I existed, after all why would he? Finally I had been noticed for doing something well.

Silently, another man appeared, praising my performance. 'Your voice reminds me of Brenda Lee' he said. 'I'm really sorry,' I replied, 'I don't know who that is.'

'She was a singer in the sixties!' he exclaimed. This man turned out to be my future father in law, although he never knew that, as he sadly passed away before I married my husband. I will always remember this moment for two reasons: firstly, because it was one of the only conversations I ever had with my father in law, and secondly, for a moment, I was someone that people wanted to talk to. I wasn't invisible and I didn't mind being seen.

As the auditorium emptied, the trumpet player from the band appeared and he sat with me. He said I had done really well. I explained that his dad had mentioned I sounded like Brenda Lee. He laughed and said, 'My dad loves his music.' We sat for ages in silence just looking at the stage, not saying anything, simply soaking up the feeling and the moment that surrounded us. For a while the world stopped; all that existed was me and the 'Trumpet Player'.

At the age of sixteen, I was still dancing at every opportunity. I wanted to be a dancer, and I wanted to get better. I moved myself to a dance school that was a bus ride away from my house. By now I had started to gain weight and was not comfortable with my body shape. However, I couldn't seem to be able to gain the control I needed over food to sort this out. Alongside this, my new dance classes were challenging. I had been the best where I was. I went from being the best to being the worst. This made me feel pretty rubbish, but I was not prepared to give up yet; I had moved schools to get better. I decided I would just work harder and that's what I did. I worked on my technique. I practiced for hours at home. My dad even put a dance barre on my bedroom wall.

My new dance teacher moved at a really fast pace. There was discipline in the classes, which I wasn't used to, and the expectations were high. The new dance school and students were so pleased to have me as they had seen me in competitions and felt I was capable of so much more. My cousins attended the dance school too, so it was lovely to be with them.

Suddenly, the one thing that made me feel free, the one thing I loved more than anything else, became difficult. This was not my plan. It didn't just become difficult, it became unmanageable.

Tap was something I particularly struggled to stay on top of, with all the steps looking and sounding the same. I couldn't pick up routines quickly. I thought it was me and that it was my fault. As the annual show approached, I realised I had no idea what I was doing. I got copies of the music and I drilled myself at every available opportunity. I would not fail at this. Again, I smiled, making light of the fact I was just slow but I'd get there!

I don't think anyone at the dance school ever knew how hard I worked behind closed doors on perfecting the routines, but also at how damaged my confidence was. My dream of becoming a dancer was being crushed; I felt it was fading into the distance because I couldn't remember the steps, which in turn hindered me being able to dance fluidly. I repeated my mantra, 'I must work harder, must listen more carefully, must remember to smile.'

I had also joined a local theatre school on a Sunday attending this alongside dance classes. It was here that I found my new freedom, singing. When I sang, I didn't have to remember to smile, I loved it. I soon discovered that the theatre school was linked to a professional company that provided the entertainment in two theatres for the summer season. Better than this, I discovered that talented students were often chosen to be in the chorus of major productions and shows throughout the summer, and would be paid for these roles. I had been there for about three weeks when, during the break, one of the teachers approached the girl I was sitting next to and offered her a part in the summer panto. She was really excited but said, 'I know I'm not going to be able to do it; we are on holiday for a month in the middle.'

I still don't know where the words came from, but from nowhere I said, 'I'll do it.' The teacher just looked at me, and there was a pause. 'I know you don't know me well, but I know I can do it! I'm a really hard worker and I'd love to do it!' To my amazement, the teacher said yes. This is one of the only times in my life I have ever felt confident enough to put myself forward, and this was the beginning of a great new adventure.

I had worked from the age of fifteen. Initially, I was a waitress in a coffee shop. I loved this job, and I did it for a few years before moving on to be a Saturday girl in New Look. Amazingly, no one noticed my lack of confidence or self-belief in either of these jobs. I was just a smiley Saturday girl. How much trouble could I get into making tea and coffee?

In New Look, my special gift unintentionally leaked out on occasions! We had to promote New Look store cards; I held the record one summer for the most store cards achieved in one day… eleven! I was always on the till because of my ability to turn on a smile and convince customers it was worth it! Of course, I did not need to work out change or money as the till did all of that for me.

Looking back now, these were possibly some of my happiest times. No stress, no reading, no learning, no academic thinking required.

At the time, it never crossed my mind that I could have stopped there; worked in a shop and been really successful. But I wanted more. I didn't know what more there was, but I knew I was capable of more and that I could push myself further. I knew that somehow I wanted to make a difference to the world, and that working in a shop was not my fate or destiny; they had yet to be decided.

I needed to go in search of more, smiling all the way of course!

A-LEVELS

My GCSE results:

A in art and drama.

B in English language, English literature, and French.

C in maths, double science, and design and technology.

D in history.

These results show that I thrived in practical subjects, whilst still working hard in the core ones to achieve everything I did! These results were not indicative of a 'swot', nor were these results indicative of a stupid person. Instead, these results opened enough doors to be whatever I decided, as long as all of my teachers wanted me on their A-level courses.

Now, in 1995, having not quite reached sixteen years old, I had to choose three A-levels. The first two were easy to pick: art and theatre studies. The third caused more of a problem, as none of the teachers wanted me on their course. Not because I wasn't willing, but because none of them believed I would cope. I had done well in French, but my teachers felt I wouldn't be able to maintain the level of work I had put in to be able to pass the A-level. English was my other grade B. I really wanted to study English language A-level, but at the time my school didn't offer it. However, my English teachers frantically tried to talk me out of English literature too. On top of this, I had no idea what I wanted to do once leaving university! I concluded that whichever third A-level I chose, I was going to struggle.

I remember my options evening clearly; I took my mum first to see Miss S. then on to Miss P., my drama teacher, who I mentioned earlier. Miss S. was full of enthusiasm for me to go to university, taking time to talk us through my options. I explained that the English teachers had discouraged me from taking English literature, and that one teacher had gone on to tell me that perhaps I should look at options other than university. Miss P. was disappointed with him, believing that I had the potential to do all of this; she told me I would be taking English literature as my third A-level. She reassured me that she would support me in any way she could.

As it turned out, English literature lessons were a new kind of hell that, up until now, I had never experienced. To begin with, there were only seven people in my class, which left me nowhere to hide. All except one from this group would go on to either Oxford or Cambridge University, all super-speedy, super-whizzy, and super-clever. Against them, I was most definitely the underdog.

Initially I did try to keep up, covering Wuthering Heights, Sylvia Plath, and Hamlet texts. I remember listening to the others debating how 'Heathcliff's personality was a reflection of the weather on the moors.' I hadn't actually read that far yet, and even if I had done, it would not be until my fourth or fifth time reading the text that I would get this abstract meaning. Despite my telling the teachers this, they would never slow down for me, and it wasn't long before I resigned myself to the fact that the teachers had not only no patience or time for me, but had given up on me. This made me start to give up on myself, aware that I had absolutely no chance of keeping up with the super-clever people in my class.

I never completely read any of the texts that I had to write about in my exams, turning instead to a combination of videos and study guides to help me piece together what I needed to know. I think I watched every version of Hamlet and King Lear that had ever been made! My mum bought me every study guide ever written on the texts, which I read from cover to cover, several times.

At the same time, I also started to struggle in theatre studies and art, because A-level subjects were suddenly more rooted in theory than they had been until now. The difference in art and theatre studies was that the teachers were more understanding; they believed in me, and they smiled back at me!

I remember a specific conversation I had with Miss P. on entering the drama studio one morning, I was asked by Miss P. to find the notes from yesterday's lesson. From my bag, I pulled out a pile of crumpled papers, English notes, drama notes, art notes, letters and books. Momentarily my cover was blown, the invisibility cloak had slipped. Miss P. made a flippant comment, meant with the best intentions, but a comment that nearly broke me! 'Jo, you really didn't strike me as an unorganized person.' I did not know how to respond. This was me. This was what I was like. I had never thought about it before. I stood and looked at her. I don't remember what I said or what happened next. I do remember feeling devastated. I felt I'd let my drama teacher down, the only one who believed in me.

I can remember telling my mum when I got home. 'Well, sometimes you come across as unorganized, but really you are not,' she said. 'You always complete homework on time. Just don't worry about it.' I was worried because it had struck a raw nerve.

Inside, I never ever felt organized; my smile had always covered this, but Miss P. had seen past it today. I'd let my guard down, and I was going to have to up my game to sort this out. I went out and bought folders, dividers, plastic wallets, highlighters, and sticky labels. I stayed up nearly all night organising my notes, determined I would not be caught out again.

I developed Obsessive Compulsive Disorder (OCD) over my schoolwork. I invented systems and had lists coming out of my ears. I spent hours and hours after each school day going back over what I had done, filing and recording in a way which looked organised just to show I was on top of it! It was exhausting, but I could not disappoint the teachers who believed in me.

Between dancing and my time spent trying desperately to comprehend what I had been taught, I was trying to organise the chaos of isolated and unrelated facts into some sort of order. I remember that I would come home from school, sleep for an hour and then crack on with homework.

I continued to escape some evenings, taking part in theatre shows as part of the chorus; Me and My Girl, Anything Goes, Best of the West End, the summer pantomime and lots more. It was these shows that got me through my A-levels. I'd stress all day, with a release from everything in the evening!

By the age of seventeen, despite knowing I was going to university to study dance, I had given up on formal dance lessons. It wasn't about giving up, it wasn't that I was afraid of hard work, it was a self-defence mechanism. Why put yourself through something that is making you feel so bad?

Meanwhile Dad made me learn to drive.

I hated the lessons and found it really difficult to follow all the verbal instructions while driving the car. There was a bigger issue though: I did not know my left from my right.

I had reached seventeen years of age not knowing

this principle. It didn't seem to matter how many times I was told which was left and which was right, I just could not remember which was which, particularly when under pressure. Learning to drive definitely meant pressure! The instructor would tell me to turn left at the end of the road and my poor brain just couldn't process what I had to do. Of course, I smiled and made light of it, but I was mortified - not knowing this principle made me feel humiliated and stupid.

I didn't feel like a typical teenager; I didn't ever go out and socialise at the pub or go out to nightclubs. I was too exhausted by the time the evenings came. Alongside this, I didn't feel old enough or confident enough. Even now, I hate going to the bar to get a drink. I can do it if I must, but I feel so overwhelmed and silly. I think this is because I like to be invisible to people who don't know me, and when asking for a drink at a busy bar you have to make yourself seen, be brash, and push yourself forward. This was something I was not comfortable with and didn't feel able to do in case I was asked a question or a comment was made that I didn't understand. I worried that I would look stupid or feel out of my depth. It was easier to just stay in.

When the A-level exams arrived, I felt physically sick, anxious, sweaty-palmed and panicky, but despite this I approached them with grim determination and quiet confidence. I had study guides full of notes. Although you couldn't take study guides into the exam, you could take the texts in. I had rehearsed timings within the exams. I knew roughly how many essay questions would be in each one, and I rigorously managed the time. Within the exams, there never seemed to be enough time to say all I needed to. I was used to this though, so I didn't think any differently about it. I just got my head down, did my best, and knew in my heart of hearts I could not have done anymore.

I passed English literature with an E which, as I proudly told my English teacher, actually stood for 'Excellent'. He had told me on so many occasions that I would never manage even a pass.

That E, and the two UCAS points that came with it, made all the difference, and saw me into my university of choice. In theatre studies, I also had to study texts and plays, and sit a three-hour exam. I read them all. My teachers pushed me, challenged me, and supported me; most importantly they believed in me and didn't give up on me. I got a B, a grade higher than I had been predicted! In art, I got a C, which I was pleased to have achieved.

While I had battled with A-levels, The Trumpet Player had been at University but our relationship of two years had grown. I wrote to him every single day, sometimes twice a day. Whenever I thought about him my face was covered with a natural ear-splitting smile, I just couldn't help myself. Mum said to me, 'I really like this trumpet player.' When I asked her why, she replied, 'Because he makes you smile, and you hardly ever smile.' She had noticed that my smiles were often fake, but was not sure what to do about it.

He had, and still has, the ability to make me smile. His unconditional love has rescued me on more than one occasion. His steady, calm, laid back nature keeps me balanced. At the end of the summer, with my results in hand, I headed off to university in Bedford to begin the next chapter of my life.

AUTUMN

Determination:

"A quality that enables someone to constantly keep forcing their way forward and improve themselves, despite it being hard work. It is never giving up on hope."

(Jo Rees, 2017)

UNIVERSITY

The day has arrived. I sit in the car, jammed between boxes, suitcases and bedding. We packed the car earlier that morning when the glistening spider webs were illuminating the pathways between shrubs and plants. As we drive to Bedford, I look out of the window and I don't feel fazed. I watch the trees as we rush past them, noticing the leaves that have started to change colour in preparation for autumn. I don't feel worried. It's an adventure; my heart starts to race and doubt begins to creep in. Perhaps I am nervous? Perhaps I am scared?

Cautiously, mum, dad and I walk through the campus trying to locate the check-in area. The blood rushes round my body as I try to make myself smaller and smaller. The lady hands me the keys and I know she is giving directions to the room; I am listening, but it is like I am underwater; everything feels muffled and I feel a bubble growing quickly around me to keep me safe and hidden. I am aware that my feet are moving as I follow dad through the winding pathways which form the main campus, but it doesn't feel real.

I do wonder why we are walking in the opposite direction to everyone else, but I don't have the words to question it. I feel scared and vulnerable, little and insignificant amongst a sea of new experiences and opportunities. There is a chill in the air as the sun begins to fade and we enter a house in the adjoining road to campus. My feet plod up the stairs, echoing my dad's footsteps, but finding my own way.

The door opens into a box room. A 2ft by 5ft camp bed fills the room, a bookshelf jammed at the end of it; a limp curtain lines an alcove hiding a wardrobe bar. The tears spring from my eyes, my mum holds me as I sob into her arms. No one speaks as Dad unloads the car, carrying a box at a time up the grubby, dingy stairway until the car is empty. Time pushes on and it's time for Mum and Dad to go, they hug me until I'm wrung out. I stand on the pavement of the barren, dirty street as I wave, fighting back another ocean of tears. 'I wanted this,'

I think. I thought that I was good enough for university.

I sit silently on the tiny bed, contemplating my fate. Mechanically taking things from a box, I begin placing them on the shelf. The four boys occupying the other three rooms of the house knock on my door and ask me to if I'd like to join them at the students' union. I can't move, I can't speak; I manage a fake smile and shake my head.

After a few hours have passed, the tears have

subsided and I manage to paint on a smile. Terrified, I walk across the campus to the student rep who had said she would take me to the students' union to meet other students. With red eyes, I knock on the door. No smiles, just the harsh greeting of 'I have been waiting, let's go.'

I stand in the corner of the students' union quietly observing the carnage unfold as more and more people pile in and the music gets louder and louder. My chest feels tight and I don't think I can keep breathing in the dark, smoky atmosphere. I'm eighteen, yet why do I feel so young, so small, so underprepared? I make my way back to my room and get ready for bed. Locking myself in and going to sleep, silently sobbing into a pillow, wondering what I have done, wishing I was back working in New Look in a safe and predictable environment.

I don't remember much of the first year, it's blurry. I know I phoned mum and The Trumpet Player every day. I know I had lectures; I know it was really hard, both socially and academically; I know I watched the trees outside my window. Eventually, the leaves fell to the floor, littering the pavements with their beauty, before disappearing into the wind.

I found living on my own challenging, mainly because I didn't seem to be able to do the simplest of things either right or well! An example of this was writing a cheque. I had never had to write cheques before and suddenly monthly cheques had to be written for rent and paying bills. I found it so difficult to write a cheque the first time, often getting completely muddled! I got the amounts wrong, the spelling wrong, and who it was written to in the wrong place. The cheque book was filled with more void cheques and blank stubs than used ones.

There was one particularly memorable incident in a book shop, when attempting to buy around £100 worth of books. I just couldn't get the cheque right – in fact, it took three attempts. I remember it so clearly because I was mortified. Firstly, I wrote the amount where I should have written who it was to. Then, I couldn't spell who it was to. Then, I couldn't remember how to write the numbers in words correctly. I was so flustered, with a massive queue of second and third year students behind me. The more I panicked, the worse it got. I made jokes and smiled to try and cover my embarrassment. I was hot, bothered, and really anxious.

Eventually I got it right, but inside I was devastated and just wanted to cry. I was eighteen and I couldn't even do a task as simple as writing a cheque. I couldn't spell the name of the shop and it was in front of me. I couldn't even remember how to write the number 'ninety'. Does it have an 'e' in it or not? Even today I'm still not sure. I was never able to bring myself to return to that bookshop.

I spent most of my university years travelling to York to stay with The Trumpet Player. York was where he was at university and it was the only place I have ever felt at home other than the Isle of Wight. I picked my modules, ensuring I had lectures on days that were all together at one end of the week so that I could have the other half of the week with him. I loved visiting him, but travelling was stressful for me. The fear of not getting on the right train, not hearing an announcement or not moving quickly enough made me anxious.

While I could plan ahead to an extent, the nature of how quickly my travel plans might need to adapt around cancellations and delays filled me with dread, in case I needed to rely on staff whose job it was to help passengers with their journey! The idea of asking for help or information was unthinkable, knowing I'd struggle to absorb whatever they told me. I knew I'd just thank them for their help and walk away none the wiser, no closer to my destination than before I'd spoken to them.

Despite planning ahead and trying to make sure I'd never have to put myself in that situation, it didn't always go to plan. I would often read the train times incorrectly, find myself waiting on the wrong platform, or even waiting for a train currently leaving from the destination I was hoping to get to, rather than from the platform at which I was standing!

The Trumpet Player had carried on with music at university, and was the musical director of the most fabulous Commitments-style band, The PPK. I occasionally sang in the band if one of the backing singers was not available. Other than the three backing singers the rest of the band were male apart from a female trumpet player, 'Scenic Route'. I took her friendship for granted. Now, without realising it, I was beginning to find true friends who were lighting up a path for me, showing me that there were other ways and options, and that maybe I deserved some of this. Scenic Route was the start of this long and tumultuous journey, and has become one of my closest lifelong friends.

My second year at university was interesting from the outset. I lived in a house with two older female students. I'm unsure how I ended up living with them, but I really liked them and they seemed to have a good time. However, I was so far out of my comfort zone living with these girls, as their whole outlook on life was different to mine. They partied hard and spent money like water, with clothes being really important to one girl in particular. I'd hoped they would be able to look after me because they were older. They were not bad people, but I was a hindrance to them. I didn't fit into their happy-go-lucky lifestyle, and my apparent serious nature did not fit with the party flavour of their house.

This was the year I left all my assignments to the last minute. I had to retake several modules as I did not complete them correctly. This was the one time in my life I can honestly say I didn't try, in fact I nearly gave up. I just wanted to get through the year. Whilst I liked the girls, living with them was so hard because I did not feel like they understood or had the patience for me. My naive nature could not cope with it, and my OCD resurfaced. I cleaned the whole house frantically every day, I got stressed if things were out of place and became obsessed with tidiness and organisation.

In amongst all this chaos I was about to find sanctuary, which came in the form of Polam Independent School…

FINDING DIRECTION

By now, I had decided that I wanted to be a primary school teacher, and next to my university campus was an independent school. One day, I plucked up enough courage to approach them. I arranged a meeting with the head teacher and asked if I could volunteer one afternoon a week, listening to children read. Very soon I became part of the furniture and lived for Wednesday afternoons.

I loved being with grown-ups (I think I missed my mum). One teacher, Mrs G. took me under her wing and counselled me on how to cope with life. I loved being with the children, particularly the children who found learning tricky. I was just drawn to them like a magnet. Ironic in some ways, I was desperate for someone to nurture and lead me gently through my learning. It hadn't occurred to me that I needed or could ask for help.

The school loved me, my dedication and my enthusiasm. I remember the first time I was asked to read a story to the class whilst the teacher saw a parent. It wasn't as easy as I thought it would be! I sat on the chair looking out into the faces of the eager minds, enthusiasm oozing from them. I held the book to the side of me and I started to read. I hesitated, struggling to read out loud and fluently. I kept stumbling over the words and did not seem to be able to get them to make sense. I was mortified at how tricky I found this. This led to me taking several books home and learning them by heart so that when it came to reading to the class, I wouldn't actually have to read the books, I would have memorised them and the children and teachers would never know this.

It was the afternoons here that helped me cope with the rest of my week, and all the stress elsewhere in my life. The main thing was that they noticed me. My twenty-first birthday fell on a volunteering day. I had told Mrs G. a few weeks earlier. I hate birthdays; they mark you getting older, and I didn't like the idea of getting older! However, the staff bought me flowers, chocolates, and a necklace. For a single day, I felt like someone; I felt like something worthwhile! I smiled real, genuine, happy smiles all day! I felt a hundred feet tall inside.

Sadly, this great feeling didn't last. The following day brought with it the lecture I dreaded each week.

This lecture was theory based, heavily comprehension based and relied on reading several chapters from textbooks. For me, this meant an evening of reading, re-reading and reading once again as I fell asleep. I'd wake in the morning with the papers and books in my hand, hoping that the sleep would have miraculously helped my brain make sense of them. It never did.

DISSERTATION YEAR

Generally, no-one noticed me as I was not the best, or even good at dancing anymore. I was self–conscious, because I had put on so much weight. I had no idea, comprehension or understanding of the current topic 'semiotics' despite reading several definitions, asking a few friends and even reading a dummies' guide to semiotics. I was terrified to ask my lecturers for help as I didn't want my cover blown. I was so scared of rejection after my experience in A-level English. I was scared that the lecturers wouldn't have patience with me, just like my English teachers. I believed that it was something I just had to get through on my own.

I was now living in a different house with people who were not on my course. Night after night I'd sit in my room, studying, reading, making page after page of notes. Even the notes didn't really make sense. I didn't know what I was looking for and because I couldn't find meaning in texts, I couldn't draw conclusions. My notes were literally whole paragraphs and chunks of text copied out. I hoped that this would somehow help it stick in my head!

The other people on the course perceived me as rich because I bought every textbook recommended. This meant I had no money to go out drinking, as it was all going on expensive books, of which I was only reading small parts. I spent hundreds of pounds on textbooks during my degree.

This was because I couldn't be under pressure from the library to return a book, knowing that if I only had a week to read it, I would understand it even less! I needed to highlight the text and make notes in my books. I needed to take my time and read them repeatedly. Somehow, this deluded me into believing that I actually understood them.

By the end of my degree, I was physically and mentally exhausted, but I passed with a 2:1. I came out alive on the outside, and outwardly I was still smiling. Inside I felt battered and broken, but still no one knew. My parents were so proud as I was the first person on either side of my family to receive a degree.

I planned to go to Winchester the following September to begin my PGCE in primary teaching. I smiled as I was awarded my degree certificate, but beneath my smile I was exhausted and self-conscious owing to my ever-growing size. My confidence and self-esteem were on the floor. I went back home and worked all summer, every hour I could, saving hard to get me through my next and final year of study.

HOORAY

ACCOMPLISHED CONCEALMENT

I arrived in Winchester on a bright autumnal morning, not knowing anyone. I can still smell that sweet, damp aroma of fresh, glassy dew drops illuminating the grass and the fading green leaves tenaciously trying to grip to the branches for a few more days, reluctant to give up, knowing at some point nature would be stronger. Brown would eventually take over, and the winds of change would finally get them. But for now, they hung delicate and vulnerable, soaking up the last rays of sun and observing the new students walking past.

I now lived in a flat with a fresher, together with another lad who was doing a master's degree. As I walked through the tree-lined streets to King Alfred's University, I thought about how far I had come. I thought back to my English literature lessons, and how I had been told that perhaps university wasn't for me. I thought back to those who had supported me to get where I was. I knew I was loved, but strangely I felt lonely. For the first time I was starting to feel responsible and like I couldn't hide anymore. I was excited and motivated about starting this course, knowing that this was what I wanted to do and that this year would fly by. It would be summer again before I had time to take in the beauty of the ever-changing seasons.

As I arrived at the lecture theatre for the first time, I walked through the door with a girl, 'Five Minutes Fast'; she and I became best friends, and still are to this day.

The days ticked by, and the lectures passed. I had developed many complicated strategies for hiding the fact that I often had no idea what was being discussed! My strategy of choice at this point was taking many highlighted, beautifully-presented notes. These were colour-coded, featuring immaculate, joined-up handwriting with matching and labelled folders. Miss P. would have been proud. Each folder had an external label detailing what was in it, which lecture it was and which subject it related to. Once on a shelf, they were a thing of beauty, a sight to behold!

IS THAT CLOCK 5 mins Fast
12
3
6
9
LECTORE ROOM

Sadly, there was nothing natural or beautiful about this order because behind this shiny, ordered exterior hid a multitude of mess, chaos, disorganisation and misunderstanding. No-one was to know that! No-one had any idea how insecure I was, how I had no confidence in my ability, and how I always felt behind.

I had also developed the strategy of asking about assignments early to get myself ahead. This gave me the maximum possible time to complete them and the best chance of passing with a semi-good mark. I could read the texts as many times as needed, draft the essay at least ten times and proofread until my eyes nearly bled.

The bit that hurt the most was that no-one ever knew how much effort went into creating an assignment. Despite all this effort, when receiving assignment feedback, an A would never come my way. Typos, errors and incorrect grammar that I would never have noticed would be identified, and internally, I would beat myself up about them.

Training to be a primary school teacher turned out to be a strategy in itself. I had found a legitimate way to improve my understanding and to develop an awareness of things I had never understood. I made my disadvantage into an advantage! Suddenly, I knew what an adjective was, because I was studying how to teach adjectives; I knew what a noun was, because I was learning how to teach what nouns were!

I quietly sat with my head down, making copious amounts of notes, learning more than I had ever learnt before. Suddenly, things I was confused about for years made sense to me. What was even better was that I was naturally a good teacher; it suited my personality, I loved performing and so much of teaching is all about performing!

My moment of realisation was when I discovered that to be a great teacher you don't necessarily need to be the best or top of the class. You could be the best at algebra, but if you don't know how to break it down and explain it, you might not make a good teacher. Teaching is very different from knowing, in fact, it can be worlds apart. At last my weakness was my strength! It didn't matter that my subject knowledge wasn't secure, because by the time I had planned a lesson I was an expert in whatever I was teaching. I knew how I had arrived at the answer, what strategies I had used to get there and what I needed to teach the children.

When children struggled I naturally spotted it, because I knew how I had hidden it for years. My students couldn't hide, because I could play the game as well as them. If they didn't learn something it wasn't their fault, but mine as the teacher. It was my responsibility to ensure that every child felt valued, supported and intelligent.

LESSONS OF LIFE

I never got less than 'excellent' for a lesson observation and I seemed to be thriving. Well, at least I was with the teaching practice part anyway! This was helped by the fact that I was in an amazing school placement with a fabulous mentor called Clare. I also met an influential newly-qualified teacher called KB. I was fortunate to have been placed here as it formed a solid foundation upon which to build my teaching experiences. From watching and talking with KB, I learnt quickly that teaching is not just about imparting knowledge. Teaching is about inspiring resilience and determination, and developing strategies so that pupils become independent learners.

KB showed me how to strengthen and build relationships with children quickly, and to this day is the most inspirational, gifted and skilled teacher I know. KB was, and still is, an outstanding teacher, and any child who comes her way is incredibly fortunate. She is a force to be reckoned with in the classroom, but has a gentle but tough approach. One that leaves you feeling like you want to do nothing less than your best, because she believes in you so fiercely.

Here I was, the master of strategies, developed in secret, able to share my special gift with eager little minds! I had arrived! Well, at least that was the case in front of the kids. They were easy to fool into thinking I was confident, organised and on top of my game. I muddled through the theory modules and managed to scrape passes, but, in all honesty, I was too exhausted inside to work any harder. It wasn't that I didn't want to learn or try (believe me I did) but I was learning so much from the children about how they learnt and the different ways to approach learning that this was all I needed at the time to get by.

It was during my PGCE that I realised just how poor my spelling was. In my flat, I had a white board that had lists on, and my housemate would often laugh at my spelling on the board. Not in an unkind way but in a 'you are so great, I just love the way you spell stuff' way. She would often say, 'I had never thought of spelling stuff that way.' She thought I did it intentionally! One of the examples of this I can remember is 'prepear'. I honestly thought that this was how you spelt 'prepare' until the day she pointed it out!

I also realised how poor my basic knowledge of number facts and general knowledge was. I wondered how I had managed to achieve anything at all so far and if I had learnt anything ever. At this point, my exterior had no cracks, but just as the autumn leaves would inevitably fall from the trees, my interior did have cracks which I was covering up and I felt worthless and stupid most of the time for not knowing, remembering, or understanding the simplest of things. I was not doing a good job of convincing myself of my worth and felt immature, self-conscious and small in social situations. Who got me through? Five Minutes Fast!

Five Minutes Fast was my rock; my constant light. She was my first true friend, other than Scenic Route; my first friend who liked me for being me. She saw through my façade and loved me still; other than The Trumpet Player, she was the first person to simply 'get' me, however, like him, she never let on that there was anything to get.

They both played the game with me; smiled with me, laughed with me, caught me when I fell, had my back when I was vulnerable and made me feel like someone worth existing.

I got married at the end of my PGCE year. More specifically, in true 'me' style I got a new job, got married, and bought a house all in the space of six weeks! I married my trumpet playing hero, who loved me unconditionally; my soul mate. I am possibly the luckiest girl in the world, to have found a love that matches my family's love for me. He chose me, he made his promises to me and I made my promises to him. It is a love which grows stronger every day that no-one else can possibly even try to compete with.

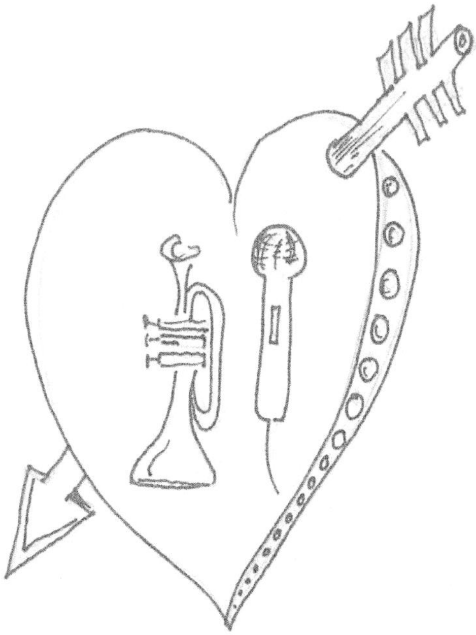

This relationship is so important to my life because his love saved me. His unconditional love is what kept me afloat and on the right path. I often wonder what would have happened to me if I hadn't found him when I did. He was a massive protective force at a time when I felt vulnerable, scared and alone.

Scenic Route, Five Minutes Fast and KB came to our wedding. Our wedding was one of the best days of my life so far. For a short while, I was lulled into a false sense of security that I was finally a grown up! I thought I had finally cracked life, but sadly this was only surface deep. My conscience had other ideas.

I thought my smile was real, but with hindsight I now know that the charade was to continue for a few more years.

WINTER

Resilience:

"A conscious action to attempt to overcome adversity, despite being forced in different directions, bouncing back to one's original form and shape."

(Jo Rees, 2017)

A VOICE STIRRED

On a cold December day, I stand looking into the eager eyes of six year olds who hang onto my every word. I understand the importance, power and influence I have as their teacher, and I will use it responsibly and with care. I know these twenty-six faces in my first proper class will never forget me, and in the last twelve weeks I have learnt that these twenty-six individuals are like snowflakes, each one unique and special. Each one must be handled with extreme care. Each one kept in the right environment to be able to admire their beauty. The lessons I plan, the activities I prepare, and the knowledge I teach will leave a lasting impression within them. Like a footprint in fallen snow, it cannot be undone, so I must tread thoughtfully but purposefully.

Enthusiasm radiates from my smile as we build trusting relationships that allow for learning and progress to be made. The days fly by and Christmas soon hangs in the air. I feel I know these children so well, I plan for their quirks and their individual needs. Every day we have fun while we learn and I feel so alive. However there are shadows in the form of 'Ice Slaves' that threaten this blissful existence. The Ice Slaves work for the 'Ice Queen', an outstanding headteacher, with years of experience and an eye for perfection. As a Newly Qualified Teacher (NQT) the Ice Slaves constantly watch and analyse my every action.

There are glass doors and windows everywhere in this school, we are always on show and always expected to be outstanding. Sometimes it's so suffocating it is hard to breathe naturally in an environment where just good is not good enough.

In the corner of my classroom is a partition door that one of the Ice Slaves constantly looks through, and is looking through now as I desperately try to get my class of children to understand symmetry. I am following a plan that has been given to me, that has been tried and tested by experienced teachers and it just isn't working. I stand looking at the snowflakes, perplexed at their confusion, thinking about the words I am using to describe the tasks I am presenting to them. Unhappy faces stare back at me; they are repeatedly making the same mistakes on the worksheets in front of them. Not one of them seems to have it. I'm feeling so negative telling them constantly to look at it again. I know they don't understand, and I know what I am doing isn't working. I look back at the plan, my eyes flick towards the glass doors and windows, as I glance back across the innocent faces. I remember wishing the glass was frosted so as to make it easier to follow my instinct.

"Stop," I command. They immediately do. "Please sit on the carpet." As they sit, I clear the desks. Shaking newspaper and placing paint pots on the tables I give instructions for them to sit quietly and listen. I take my seat in front of them and demonstrate how to make a butterfly picture, painting on one side, and then gently folding it in half. We spend the next twenty minutes creating butterfly pictures with beautiful symmetry.

The children talk animatedly, desperately trying to create intricate and complex patterns, observing and pointing out the symmetry they see. I am aware that an Ice Slave could walk past at any moment, peer into my classroom and question my actions. If they do, my plan is to cautiously smile at them, hoping that they will reflect it back and the ice will melt.

The windows are not frosted; Ice Slaves are continuously walking past, peering through but not entering, with the glass radiating a coldness that is palpable. Inside, I feel anxious at what they might say later, momentarily the ground beneath me turns to ice and shatters, but somehow, I am still standing. No matter how hard they try, they don't seem to be able to override the proud feeling that pours out of me. I have thought on my feet and am enabling a lesson which could have been a disaster, to become a success.

I observe the children, every single one of them is excited and on task, doing what was asked of them. Thirty minutes pass and together, calmly and productively we pack away, quickly returning the classroom to its original clinical state.

The children sit in a circle and one by one stand up and explain where the symmetry is on their picture and describe how and why it was there.

I reach a small girl with a bob. This little girl is sobbing, 'I've done it wrong Mrs Rees, I forgot to fold it in half, I have not got any symmetry on my picture.' There is silence, 'you might not have folded your picture in half, and you might not have any symmetry on that piece of paper but you have learnt what symmetry is today because you know your picture doesn't have any.'

A smile slips across her face and quickly reaches her eyes and makes them sparkle. 'Does anyone have any ideas how we can fix this picture?' I ask. Twenty-five hands shoot up. Many of the children shout 'put another piece of paper on top or if you stick another piece to it, then that will be the line of symmetry. These children are on fire, so engaged and excited about their learning. We finish talking through the rest of the pictures, as I calmly send them off to lunch. I am left with a beaming smile, feeling magical. What an amazing lesson!

My smile doesn't last for long. An Ice Slave appears from behind a glass door, and she is clearly not happy. 'Was painting on the plan?' she questions. 'Well they didn't get it,' I reply in my defence, 'but they do now. It was an amazing lesson and they all get it.' She replies with, 'My advice to you is to never get paints out in the morning again, you were lucky the Ice Queen didn't see you. Here, we believe mornings are for learning and structure. Painting is for the afternoons.'

I respond meekly, feeling disheartened, chastised and wanting the frozen ground to swallow me up, but also experiencing a strange sensation; it is faint but I think I'm feeling a bit of a fire in my belly that could melt the ice. I want to argue. I want to shout. I want to shout that they were learning. I want to scream 'I know what I am doing,' but my inner voice is squashed by years of feeling small, insignificant and ultimately stupid for not getting things quite right. The self-doubt swamps me, and quickly extinguishes any rising flames. Perhaps I do not understand the principles of teaching and learning? Perhaps I should have tried harder in the theory lessons? Maybe I am doing this all wrong?

The school is driven by a passion and determination to get results. My passion is to develop rounded children. I decide I will try to protect the snowflakes from being destroyed. I constantly feel under threat and whilst I feel confident that I know where I need to take my children, the Ice Slaves regularly make me doubt myself, regularly make me feel little, and leave me questioning my judgement and the gut instincts which drive me on a daily basis.

There is a chill in the air as we have our final meeting before the winter break. One of the Ice Slaves is discussing setting the children by ability. My head is screaming at her, 'No, no, no!' The idea of setting feels barbaric and it strikes a raw nerve with me.

My dad did not pass his 11 plus, so did not go on to grammar school. He lived the rest of his life believing he was not clever or intelligent. This failure at eleven sent a message, whether intentionally or subconsciously to the children that they were not good enough. By separating the children and setting them, we were already highlighting the difference in their ability. At six this was surely too young? I want to verbalise my thoughts, but I'm too scared, lacking not only confidence but feeling my voice would never be loud enough to be heard.

On returning to school after the Christmas break, I find myself in front of a different group of children for both English and maths. The setting by ability has happened. I really wanted the low attaining set, but I am given the high attaining classes for both subjects, mostly due to my being a NQT. I am only just beginning to understand the principles of teaching and learning but if the Ice Queen and Ice Slaves stopped for a moment to look beneath the surface, they would have noticed and seen that I had built up confidence, self-esteem and self-belief in all of my lowest attaining children, to the point that they were making rapid and accelerated progress. The gap was closing, despite having only taught them for twelve weeks.

It is a battle I know I will not win, so I am going to embrace the top set, knowing the Ice Queen and the Ice Slaves feel this is a safe bet. I get my head down and get on with it. Even to this day I have always put my unhappiness to one side, working hard and doing the best I can.

Times goes on and I feel demoralised. The enthusiasm I had a year ago is fast losing its sparkle, slowly being replaced by a dull, artificial light that is the norm in so many others within this school. Meanwhile, I am repeatedly told by parents that they feel their children are thriving in my class, but their warmth can't reach me. I continue to smile on the surface despite internally feeling hopeless.

As my NQT year ends I make a decision. This school is just not for me. Constantly being on show, doing things how they have 'always been done', and ticking boxes as the conveyer belt travels past is not what I thought teaching was about. While I agree with the school, that progress is the most important thing, I know first-hand that it is how that progress is reached that matters. If the process means drilling and breaking children just to achieve the necessary progress in them, then I know that I cannot be a part of it.

I am driven by the individual faces. I see sad faces, happy faces, unsure faces, neglected faces. Every face has a story, each one different and this story affects how they will perform on any given day. Everyone needs to fail in order to learn, but if this failure is not surrounded by some success we will naturally give up. I knew this because tap dancing, which I had loved and I had been good at, had suddenly become too difficult and the constant failures had outweighed the success. Too much failure, resulted in no enjoyment, which made me give up.

On my final day at this school, as I walk away, I reflect on everything I have been taught and have learnt, both about the children and myself. I am grateful for my time in this school and for the role the Ice Queen and her Ice Slaves played, because they awoke something in me that I did not know was there. I discovered I have views and opinions on teaching, and how it can be done. I have discovered the sort of teacher I wish to be. There is more than one way to find success, and to move children forward I had to believe it and follow my instinct. I just needed to develop the confidence to start acting on these opinions because some of them were valid. Thanks to the Ice Slaves I could finally see that I had a voice, I just needed to find a way to get it out and use it to make a difference.

HELLO
HELLO
HELLO
HELLO
HELLO

THE REAL WORLD

While I completed my NQT year, I was also a newlywed and I had to acclimatise to living with my husband and supporting ourselves. I began to realise I was hopeless with dates, times and places. I could remember them in isolation, but couldn't seem to connect them together. I constantly double booked myself, got the wrong times for appointments or completely missed appointments.

I vividly remember one Friday reminding myself I had a bride-to-be and her bridesmaids coming to visit me on Saturday morning for a hair practise. I loved doing complex up do hairstyles and had done many of my friends' wedding hair. I reminded myself all day on the Friday.

On Saturday morning when I got up, I said goodbye to my husband who was going to work, and decided to treat myself to a haircut. I phoned the hair salon and managed to get an appointment for an hour later. Half an hour later as I was leaving the house, I opened the front door to a potential bride-to-be and her bridesmaids. 'Oh hello,' I say, 'I was just looking to see if you were coming!' I let them in, and then ran upstairs to cancel my own hair appointment. Unfortunately, this wasn't the only time, and I have done similar things like this many times throughout my life.

Because of this incident, I bought myself a calendar and started writing lists for everything. I had lists everywhere. A list for remembering to put the washing on, remembering to get the car tax, remembering to post a letter, and remembering what I had to do today. After years of forgetting things and making what felt like stupid mistakes, I had developed a strategy I was confident would handle this problem. It isn't a joke when I say at the start of my book I generally forget the thing I need the most!

My new job was at my local primary school teaching Year 3. I still loved teaching, and remained passionate in wanting to make a difference to children's lives. As I started this year of teaching, I once again formed relationships quickly with children and families, and quickly slotted into the existing staff team.

I had a lively class of thirty-two children as my form group and the most amazing teaching assistant in the world, known as 'Super Star.' This school also set for English and maths. It was how it had been at this school for several years. Each morning, I taught lots of different children. However I got the set no-one else wanted, which was ironically the set I was desperate to get my hands on. I got the lowest attaining children in Year 3 and Year 4. Twenty-two of them. This also meant I got all the teaching assistants.

It was here that I worked with and met 'Understated'. She is known as 'Understated' because she is exactly this. She didn't always shout from the rooftops, but what she did do was to instigate holistic professional conversations that moved practise forward. She was so knowledgeable about special needs and behaviour management in particular, and I learnt so much about developing children's confidence and self-esteem from her.

We had a blast in our set; we did things practically, working on what we already knew. We did lots of overlearning, using routines such as flashcards, bingo and consolidating basic skills, for example, knowing which letters were vowels. We did the vowel rap every day. I had one display in my classroom that showcased outstanding work that reflected effort and new learning, no matter how small the improvement might have been.

The rest of my displays were filled with scaffolding such as word banks, vocabulary walls, maths knowledge and questions. They were interactive, but by no means perfectly laminated.

I thrived on working with children with additional needs. My expectations were so high and I pushed those minds hard, though never ever in to the panic zone. I ensured that all the pupils remained in their maximum learning zone, tailoring my planning to their needs and building on their existing knowledge. At the end of the year, my set had performed as well as the set above. Every single child had made exceptional progress in reading.

I had not made a secret about the fact I enjoyed working with pupils with special educational needs. I saw it as my own personal mission to be their advocate, to be their voice, and to make sure they felt good about themselves. At the time, I didn't know why, but I didn't want them to be invisible. I wanted to empower them to feel equal, and I felt I had to be their voice in an attempt to protect them.

Every time I taught them, I thought of my dad, having lived much of his life believing he was unintelligent, because he had found school so difficult. The more I learnt about teaching and learning and the more courses I went on, the more I felt confident that my dad was dyslexic, and that if he had been taught by different teachers in the right way, he would have achieved more academically.

I did not wish for the children in my class to be examples of history repeating itself. The children I taught would know they were amazing, would know when they had made progress, and would not feel bad about themselves. I strove to protect them, inspire them and at the same time develop their independence. My teaching at this point was not based on theory but on gut instinct. There were no Ice Slaves at this school, in fact it was the complete opposite. It was a school that fostered independence, and viewed all children and families holistically.

The difficulty was I had set unrealistic expectations of what I wanted to achieve. I spent hours and hours planning, researching and trawling the internet for ideas. The energy this effort was consuming was not sustainable in the long term. The only way to go was down!

Just as I was starting to gain a bit of confidence and smile a little more without trying, everything changed in both by personal and professional life. I fell pregnant. I was so excited, but as many other women have experienced, I had a miscarriage. With my self-belief at the time, I secretly thought that this was my fault. I genuinely believed the bad stuff, and if you tell yourself enough times you are stupid you start to believe it, which only serves to drive you to a self-fulfilling prophecy.

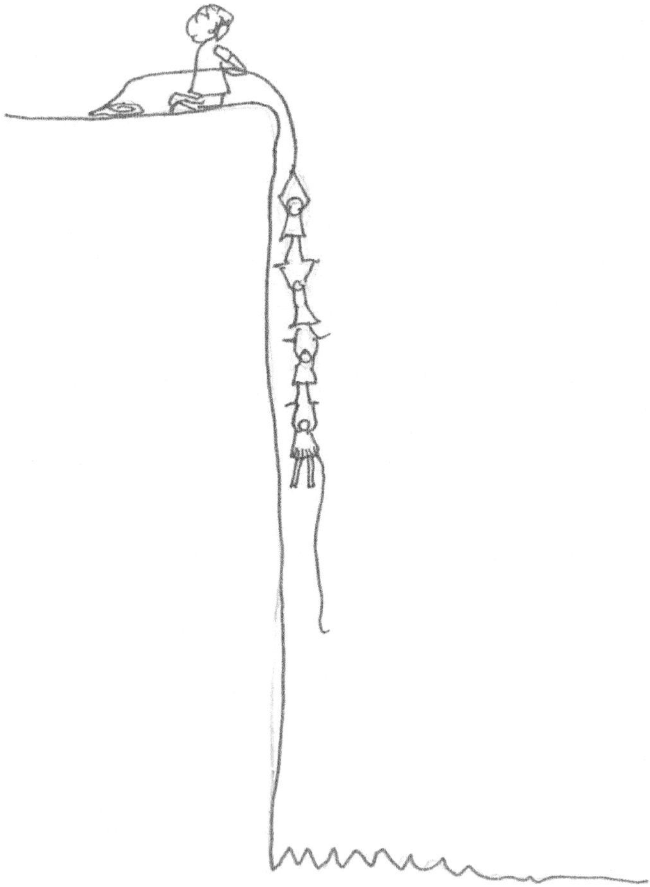

At the same time, the school did a mid-year restructuring and because I was viewed as a strong teacher and appeared to be coping well, I lost 'Super Star' to a failing class. I still had a teaching assistant, but she wasn't the same. I was doing so well, looking confident on the outside, although I just didn't feel it on the inside. 'Super Star' had become my rock, we second-guessed each other and knowing how hard I was working, she always had my back! It wasn't bad with the new teaching assistant, but she needed lots more support and she did not have the same rapport with the children.

I had become a victim of my own success, and although I might have looked as if I was coping on the outside, inside I was so fragile because I didn't really believe in myself. 'Super Star' offered me the reassurance I needed to keep going.

I was twenty-three, but I still felt sixteen inside and felt invisible. I began scratching my face again, which had been my way of showing what I couldn't say. I couldn't articulate how I felt, although this time my anxiety wasn't about me, but instead was over my children, and by MY children, I mean my class. I knew I would be unable to sustain the rate of progress I had planned with this change of TA. For a class of children who each had significant individual needs, they mostly all made good progress, but the perfectionist in me felt that this was not good enough.

At the start of my third year teaching, I was made SENCo (Special Educational Needs Coordinator), having proven that I could get results. My personal passion and mission at wanting to support and help make a difference to pupils' lives and education stood me in a good position to begin to make a positive difference. Like some sort of silent campaigner, I began the task of actually getting children put on the SEN (Special Educational Needs) register. The register grew and grew, to the extent that the governors asked me to attend a school governors' meeting to explain why the numbers had suddenly grown!

I got on well with the SEN Governor and I had a pre-meeting with her, in which she asked me many questions. I responded with a fierce determination, feeling like Erin Brockovich. I knew dates of birth, current attainment levels, addresses, dyslexic screen scores, chronological ages and reading ages for every single child on the register. They were my children and I would fight to protect them. I suddenly felt able to express my opinion but after suppressing it for so long, I felt like I had to fight and shout to get my voice heard.

I felt I often made myself look silly because of my passionate outbursts and lack of being able to back everything up with theory. I managed to survive the governors' meeting without too many tricky questions. They were happy with the answers I gave and the SEN register stayed as it was, but on the inside, I took a few internal blows because I was still so fragile and yet still no-one knew.

Amongst the bad things, some good things were happening, but I didn't see any of it. I was doing well at work, hence the change of TA, however, it was my unrealistic expectations of myself that saw me defining myself only by the negative things. This became clear when I studied for a nurture group qualification.

Nurture groups support vulnerable children. They are resources to bridge gaps in developmental learning, aimed at children who have low confidence, low self-esteem and a lack of self-belief, often due to issues with attachment. Attachment theory is about how we, as humans, bond with our primary caregivers.

Ideally, this bond is created at birth, but sometimes, for many reasons, this natural process can be hindered. If this relationship is not established and secure, it can cause a person to develop difficulties with confidence, self-worth and with managing their behaviour and emotions. A damaged or incomplete attachment will impact a person's life negatively and unless identified and supported is likely to remain with a person throughout adulthood.

I loved this course. Firstly, because I was on it with 'Understated' and 'Super Star', and what a team we were, referring to ourselves as Charlie's Angels.

Secondly, I discovered that the theories of attachment were actually very interesting! I understood it immediately, and knew how I could make it better for children, seeing opportunities to break the cycle, supporting the parents as well as the children.

The importance of mentioning this course here is that the course deliverer made a passing comment which stuck with me, and was the start of me recognising that I needed to change my thinking: 'Do you know that for every negative event that happens in a day you need at least three positives to cancel it out?'

Owing to the unrealistic, unmanageable and ridiculous expectations I placed upon myself, everything seemed negative, but I had started to look for the positives to cancel out my negatives. I had a long, long way to go, but I could see how he was right. I could see how this would affect a child's thinking just as it had affected mine. My negatives were situations where I felt out of my depth, or had failed, which was most of the time, because deep down I always felt I was stupid. I popped this to the back of my mind after a few weeks as life took over again, but I knew that somehow, I needed to change my mind set and change my thinking.

It was at this time that I fell pregnant again.

Everything was about to change and go in a direction I could never have predicted. I had absolutely no idea what was coming, and no idea that shortly I would find the brightest of lights that would steer me away from the cold spiral of self-destruction and turn me in a completely different direction. What was to come would push me out of my comfort zone to a place closer to feeling free. For now though, life took over and pretending to live was all I could do, because it was all that I knew.

THE IMPORTANCE OF INSTINCT

I was so excited about having a child. This showed on the outside, but no-one knew how fragile I was on the inside. I was still finding it hard to articulate when I didn't understand something or to ask for help, which I still believe stemmed from years of being too scared to ask and living in fear of looking stupid in front of people. I had reached the point where I was even worrying about asking questions in case the questions themselves were stupid, feeling like I was beginning to lose all power of speech when talking about myself. This really came into play when I was at the doctors. I felt intimidated by their knowledge, feeling inferior to them. I just felt like I wasn't good enough.

So many times, I went to the doctors and came out with either not having asked what I went in for, or coming out without what I even needed, finding myself increasing unable to speak rationally and losing all power of logic!

I spent a fair bit of time in hospital between the ages of twenty-two and twenty-six, breaking both my arms at the same time. I also had suffered from a grumbling appendix, being admitted to hospital three times before they finally took it out. My poor husband spent a fair proportion of our first years of married life sitting next to me in a chair while I laid in a hospital bed!

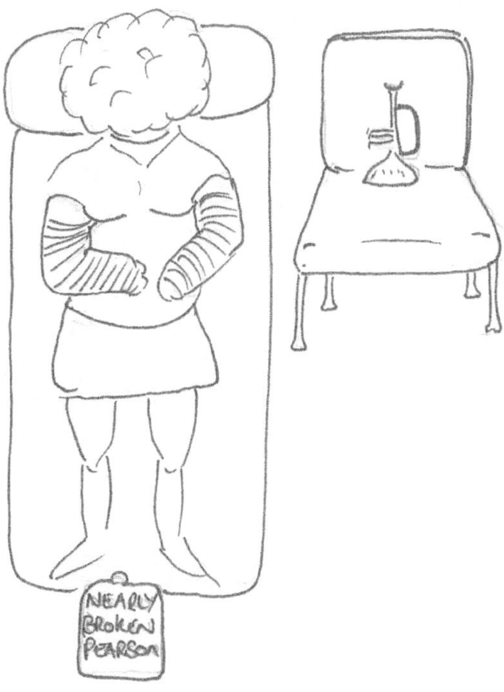

Our son was born when I was twenty-six, but I didn't feel twenty-six on the inside. Emotionally I still felt like a teenager. We were left alone for long periods of time as I laboured. I told the midwife on several occasions I was scared and that it really hurt. I had wanted an epidural the moment I arrived in hospital, but owing to how my labour was progressing I was not able to have one. I spent much of the night laid on my back, so consequently lay still. After a long, hellish night, which was no doubt was even worse for my helpless on-looking husband, the baby's heartbeat on the monitor indicated him to be in distress and he was delivered via emergency caesarean section (C-section).

When I held my 8lb 12oz baby boy for the first time the rush of emotions and love I felt for him were out of this world. Any new parent will describe it in the same way. Alongside this crazy rush of emotions, I also knew he wasn't ok. I don't know why or how, but I just instinctively knew. I am really intuitive about people and emotions, and can read body language and subtext like a book. It has been commented on many times how I am able to interpret unsaid words.

For the first few hours he did seem fine, he fed and he slept. I was exhausted, but I did not want to take my eyes off him. This was my first child and perhaps that is what all new parents naturally do.

Looking back, it was more than that. Something wasn't right and I just knew it. I didn't have the words or confidence to articulate this, and having never had a baby before I had no experience to draw on.

I felt intimidated by the midwives and was worried to say anything in case it was wrong. While I do not mind being wrong, after years and years of feeling stupid and hiding from myself in a bid to keep my weaknesses hidden, it was still easier to keep my thoughts to myself.

My baby boy was about four hours old when things started to deteriorate. My husband had, by now, left to go and get some well-earned sleep. My baby just didn't look right, he just wasn't happy and was now vomiting. While I knew it didn't feel right, how on earth could I tell a midwife this? They would just think I was an insane, neurotic mother. In reality, I knew my feelings were based on nothing other than my gut instinct.

It turned out that instinct was pretty good when it came to parenting. An hour later, after my baby had vomited yet again, he was rushed to the neonatal unit where they discovered he had a severe chest infection. He was in an incubator for three days and had to have antibiotics.

Every cloud has a silver lining and owing to my baby's visit to the neonatal unit, I met another one of my closest friends, 'Nomad.' The 6lb baby next to my baby boy had been born on the same day, but was four weeks premature. Our babies were in the neonatal unit whilst Nomad and I were on the maternity ward.

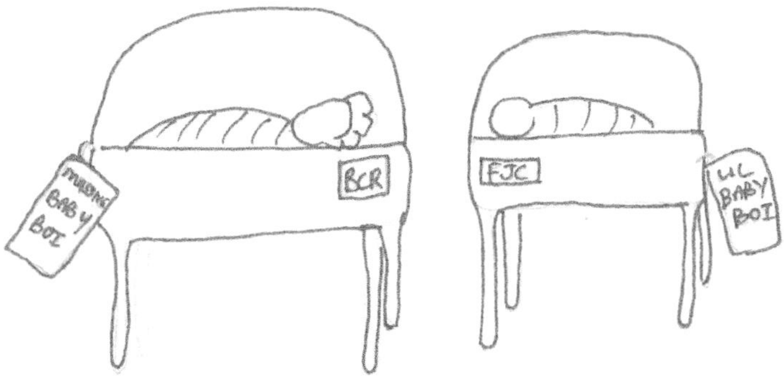

Every morning we would sit and have breakfast together looking at all the other mums who had their babies with them, longing to hold our babies freely. We would then take the lift down to the unit and sit and stare through the glass of the incubators both saying silent prayers that our boys would be okay. My boy looked ridiculous next to his new, very small best friend laying still in the incubator next to him.

When I look back to this experience, I give myself a silent smile because I knew he wasn't okay the minute he came out. I just didn't have the words to express this to anyone. I could read his needs like a well-read book, although ironically, I had not read any books about parenting! I knew what all his cries meant. I really got him. The difficulty was that in the back of my mind was a nagging thought which overpowered all the positive ones. I genuinely believed that the reason he had to be delivered by a caesarean was my fault. It was my fault he went to special care, because I couldn't get him out. Also, I had known he wasn't okay and hadn't told anyone. I felt like I had failed at what nature had designed me to do.

At the time, I never thought to question what happened during labour. All I needed to know was he was in distress and they managed to get him out because I couldn't do it.

When my son was six months old I attended a playgroup. Here I met the one person who has had the biggest impact on my life after my husband. My brightest light and my harshest critic. She was my revolution and is my 'Unbiological Sister'. 'Unbiological' juggled two children, had a husband who worked away, looked after a field with four horses, worked part time, was outwardly confident and made it all look so easy. Our friendship started to grow steadily, meeting once a week, getting to know each other.

Through my experiences, I had learnt that I often needed to do something once to settle my often incorrect expectations and fears! For instance, I was terrified of horses. I say 'was' - I am no longer terrified of horses, thanks to Unbiological. She had several horses, and refused to let me be terrified of them. One day she caught me off guard, and before I knew it I was actually riding a massive horse!

Initially, I couldn't get on. Unbiological had told me how to mount the horse solely with words. Looking back now, it was another instance like the hundreds of others when I had found myself unable to process what someone was trying to explain when it was given as a set of verbal instructions. As was so often the case, I was unable to piece together what she was asking me to do. However, after ten minutes of trying to process her verbal instructions, I was finally brave enough to come out and say, 'show me - I need to see it! Then I'll be able to do it!' After a quick demonstration, I got straight on the horse. Unbiological knew I had it in me, and she wouldn't stop until she had brought out the best in me. Slowly she was changing my mind-set, and showing me there was always another way to get things done.

With Unbiological came a new group of friends. I never felt more out of my depth than when I was with them, and yet I loved being with them. They were amazing people with varied and very successful jobs, and one of the things I loved about them most was their confidence. I often sat in awe and wonder soaking up the confidence that oozed out of them as they discussed their everyday lives. Strangely at the same time, their confidence made me feel uneasy and intimidated.

Despite this feeling, I loved being surrounded by their self-assured ideas and opinions. I couldn't believe that I was becoming part of this group. I felt honoured and privileged, like I had been chosen, even though I felt I had nothing I could offer them in return. In the beginning, I was very quiet during the social events we had together, never believing I had much of any value to say. I would sit on the side-lines and watch them in action, but all the time watching them inspired me to challenge expectations and to challenge myself.

When I fell pregnant with my second child, my first was only a year old. I was so excited until I hit twenty weeks. I then began to panic about how I would 'get it out'. I desperately did not want another C-section, but had no idea how I was going to manage to give birth naturally. Owing to my previous C-section, I was under the care of a consultant and at twenty-two weeks I had to go and see him. I was dreading it owing to still feeling intimidated by medical professionals, and to make matters worse I went to this appointment on my own as my husband was at work.

After leaving the consultant's office, I got in the car and cried and cried. The doctor used words and language I did not understand. He talked over me to the nurse as if I wasn't there, and basically said that I would have to have another C-section if my baby wasn't born by thirty-nine weeks, as my son had been big and this baby was bound to be bigger. He also asked me if my baby boy was developing normally, as my notes of previous labour showed that he had had a flat heartbeat at times.

I was mortified and felt devastated by what they were saying to me. I didn't understand much of what had been said, but my lack of confidence stopped me questioning what they were saying and I knew that was entirely my own fault. I cried not because I was sad about what had been said, but because I was frustrated with how I was handling it, reaching the point of feeling completely overwhelmed. I now realise that it is not a weakness, but actually a strength. It shows I care for myself; it also shows I have reached a point where I am not going to just accept it anymore and I look for a way to take back control.

I contacted my lovely community midwife and explained what had happened with the consultant. I asked if she would be able to get my notes from the hospital and talk me through my first labour so that I could understand it. I needed to understand it, for me, knowing that if I could make sense of what had gone wrong, maybe I could change it this time.

The midwife came and I was armed with my mother-in-law as a second pair of ears. I asked question after question. The midwife patiently took me through everything that I had wanted answers to for so long. It turned out that my son was particularly large. He was 10 days late, which I knew, but babies who are late apparently often get in distress. Alongside this, he was also trying to come out back-to-back and face first. This was an explanation apparently for all the pain I had experienced.

I was astounded to discover that I would not have been able to control any of this. In fact, it actually had nothing to do with me. With this in mind, I was determined to have a natural delivery this time. I didn't read books, but I watched TV programme after TV programme about giving birth. I saw both how I didn't want to do it, but also built up my own picture of how I would like to do it. When I entered labour this time, I would be prepared; like everything else in life my solution was to be one step ahead of the game.

As well as watching loads of TV programmes, I talked to everyone I could about their experiences of birth. My nan had had three children and felt her most relaxing delivery was the one where she walked and walked and walked. She explained she had given birth to my auntie at home, and how she did laps around the kitchen table! She didn't sit during the labour period but kept upright and paced through each contraction. For the last two weeks of my pregnancy I walked everywhere and only sat on a birthing ball. This was not about having the perfect labour, this was about me doing all I could to give myself the best possible chance of giving birth on my own.

When I finally went into labour, ten days late, I walked through every contraction and rocked on the birthing ball in-between contractions. Walking through the pain, I was visualising walking closer to holding my baby in my arms. When I got to hospital I was disappointed to discover I was not as far ahead as I had hoped, and the midwife informed me she would be back shortly to remove me from the labour ward and put me on a maternity ward as I was a way off being ready to deliver. I told her I didn't want to be in bed. I wanted to stand up, but still she insisted on laying me down. As she left the room I said, 'I think I need to push'. She turned, smiled and said, 'We are a way off that yet, just try to get some sleep.'

Goodness I felt stupid! Having never delivered a baby before I felt sure the midwife was right. Thirty minutes later, however, I had a baby girl in my arms weighing 7lb exactly. It turned out I was right. More importantly, I had done it. I had given birth and I had told the midwife I knew I was ready. She had ignored me, but what mattered was that I had verbalised it and achieved it all on my own. When it had finally happened, I was ready and when it happened I coped much better. My daughter had entered the world the way a baby should.

Although it was hard work, I was enjoying being a mum. I loved watching my children learn something new. Life was super busy going out and about with them, to the park, on long walks, to the beach, often with Unbiological or Nomad and our children. We started lots of our own traditions including an Easter treasure hunt in a local wood. We would hide chocolates and lollypops and the eager little hands would search and find them.

My son was turning into a sparky two-year-old. He loved to talk, and was so articulate about the things he had done, experienced and seen, and his passion for life radiated from him. He was a caring and sensitive soul and was always noticed for being kind, considerate and thoughtful of others. He asked thousands of questions a day - in fact, my son's language was exceptional for such a small child. He was so interested in finding out about how things worked and was brilliant at problem solving. He rarely sat still, and while I had noticed that he didn't like looking at books, I wasn't worried as this would surely come with time.

After all, I told myself, he was a boy, and was too busy digging in the mud, making sandcastles on the beach or building tall towers with bricks to stop long enough to share a story. I read him stories every night and he would talk about the pictures and makes connections to his own experiences.

Time was passing quickly and my husband and I established a covers band; music is such a huge part of our lives. We rehearsed fortnightly and did the occasional gig, including weddings, parties, summer balls and school fete entertainment. I was one of the singers and my husband of course played the trumpet. The band enabled me to build more friendships. 'Solid and Reliable' was a fellow singer and listening to the trials and tribulations in her life always made me feel a little better. There always seemed to be a drama in her life, which far outweighed any small trauma I felt I might have been having. She is one of the best listeners I know, and I always feel better after a cuppa with her.

There was also 'Always There', a friend who I wish I could give more time to, although her life is as hectic as mine, if not more so. When it really counts and matters however, we are there for each other.

I had gone back to work part-time around my children as a SENCo at the same local primary school, but I was becoming bored. There seemed to be no challenge anymore, and whilst I loved my job I felt like I had stopped learning. A job was advertised in the local paper for a Specialist Teacher of Dyslexia. I didn't have the qualification, but I decided I could get one. I applied and was appointed and with that, a new journey was about to begin.

THE REVELATION

I am not sure why, with two babies now aged three and one, that I had thought it would be a good idea to change jobs. The manager that appointed me at the time believed in me and saw my potential. At the age of twenty-eight I became the Teacher in Charge of one of four specialist dyslexic provisions within my Local Authority. As a part of accepting the job I had to get a formal qualification in dyslexia. I selected a Postgraduate Certificate in Dyslexia and Literacy, through Dyslexia Action. It was a year-long distance learning course, with the majority of learning delivered online. There was, however, a four-day introduction to the course held near London. This meant leaving my two babies with my husband. These four days turned out to be an extraordinary road to self-discovery for many reasons, with an unexpected outcome as well as an interesting start on the journey to discovering the real me.

I joined the dyslexia course thinking I knew lots about it, but it turned out I knew very little. Concerned parents and teachers had often described what they considered to be dyslexia to me. I heard time and time again things like: 'They confuse b and d and they read what they think they see, reversing letters and words', 'They are slow readers', and 'They don't seem to be able to learn their spellings.'

The first revelation was that dyslexia is a spectrum of differences and difficulties that can be experienced in varying amounts. It is like an iceberg; the difficulties we see with reading, spelling and writing are on the surface but these are only a symptom of underlying difficulties with (amongst others) auditory processing, working memory, auditory sequencing, and phonological processing. These difficulties affect how we process and store words and sounds in our brain. This also affects how we remember them, and how we can retrieve them when needed. Alongside this, there may be difficulties with directionality, orientation of letters, sequencing, ordering of letters and numbers, and making connections with prior learning. Any, and all, of these can impact on a person's confidence and self-esteem, which can then become the biggest barrier to their learning.

On arrival at the course venue, I remember walking into a room full of about one hundred people sitting around huge circular tables. I chose to sit in the middle, off to one side. I estimated the average age of the people in the room to be around forty, yet here was I at just twenty-eight, feeling completely out of my depth. The people on the table I had chosen to sit down at started to chat, introducing themselves to one another.

I watched, considering whether I should just bolt from the room or give it a few more minutes before admitting I didn't think I could do this. One of the women on the table disturbed me from my thoughts asking my name and where I came from. I wondered if perhaps I was in some strange gameshow? Unfortunately, I was brought back to reality as the room burst into rapturous applause. A lady entered the room from the back and walked towards the screen at the front of the room. I joined in the clapping, watching everyone else. I was smiling of course, nodding and looking like I knew what and who we were clapping for.

After a moment's pause we were introduced to the most inspirational lady. She was one of the writers of the Dyslexia Institute Literacy Programme (DILP), which was central to the course. Everyone in the room appeared to know who this lady was, apart from me. She was apparently a key figure within Dyslexia Action. I would have known this if I had only joined the website and managed to get onto

'Moodle'.

Moodle was the online learning tool we would be using to complete the next year of the course. Everyone appeared to have already registered. I hadn't because, despite trying, I couldn't follow the written instructions and I needed someone to show me. I was secretly feeling a bit hopeless and useless, because I hadn't managed to do this already, and here on day one I already felt like I was falling behind.

I sat listening to this inspirational force who was full of anecdotes of teaching literacy in prisons to both adults and teenagers. She started saying the letters of the alphabet, or rather the sounds that the letters of the alphabet make, one by one. As she said them she wrote them on the board and divided them into two groups. Once she got halfway through she stopped and asked who knew what she was doing. Half the group raised their hand. As she continued, more and more people put their hand up. I was frantically trying to look for the secret code to work out why the letters were placed on different sides, but I couldn't crack it. She finished and I still had no idea. Eventually she explained that she was dividing the letters into voiced and unvoiced sounds.

Voiced and unvoiced sounds. I had never heard of them before! I learnt that some letter sounds are created using your voice, for example 'a' and 'i'. Whereas 'h' and 's', for example, are created by pushing air through your lips or teeth, and so are called unvoiced. Pure sound is when you say a letter without the 'uh' after it. For example, 'r' is actually 'rrrrrr' not 'ruh' and 'f' is 'ffffff' not 'fuh.' These things are of paramount importance if you are dyslexic and are an essential starting point in being able to read and spell successfully. It is vital you do not add the 'uh' sound at the end of individual letter sounds as this will affect your ability to read or spell accurately. For example, the word 'cat,' is only made complicated by adding the 'uh' sounds. When adding an 'uh,' it sounds like 'cuh-ah-tuh.'

The next thing the magic lady did was write an 'a' on the board. 'The sound is aah' she commands, 'shout words at me that begin with 'a' - 'ant', 'apple', 'animal', 'another'. People are shouting from all over the room. I began to think to myself that I can do this. I pluck up the courage and shout, 'alien!' The room goes quiet. The lady replies, 'yes, it begins with 'a' but listen again to the sound it is making. We want words with the short 'a' sound. Alien begins with the long 'a' sound.'

Words continue to fly. I sit stunned. It does make the 'a' sound surely? It was at this point I began to think I really can't do this, but more than anything I began wondering why I was unable to hear the difference?

I sat, wanting to fade into nothing, palms sweating, wishing upon wishing I was not in this room a hundred miles from home, putting myself through an uncomfortable living hell all over again. I felt I was surrounded by intelligent people who knew what they were doing. I, however, didn't feel intelligent because I hadn't realised until today that there were two different sounds for the letter 'a'.

A memory popped into my head: no wonder I could never tell the difference between 'our,' 'hour', and 'are' when I was at middle school. Perhaps this was the reason why I thought they were the same word? Perhaps I had a difficulty with phonological awareness? I quickly learnt that a difficulty with phonological awareness meant that dyslexics struggled to process the subtle differences in sounds. We are blissfully unaware of the differences, until one day when we discover it by being wrong and the differences are pointed out to us. This, I can tell you from experience, is not good for a person's self-esteem, having happened to me too many times to mention during my life, let alone remember. Incident after incident of mishearing and not understanding came to mind.

Once this task had finished, the lady pulled two sparkly gift bags from under the table, as if she was a magician. She shook them. 'These sparkly bags are representative of magnificent brains. Let's look at what's inside these brains. Before I open them, I want to make it very clear each brain has been exposed to identical information.' She opened the first bag. She pulled out a clear box with computer disks in it. The disks were colour coded, all lined up, beautifully tidy, labelled and in alphabetical order. She opened the other bag. Just as if it were Mary

Poppins' carpet bag, she pulled out string, a couple of disks, Blu-Tack, labels, dividers, and an empty box. 'So,' she said, 'what can you tell me about these brains?' There was a brief pause, before hands flew up and millions of explanations came flying towards her.

What this analogy exquisitely demonstrated was that the brains of dyslexic people receive and process information in a different way to the brains of people who are not dyslexic. Non-dyslexic brains can file neatly and link information in a logical and ordered way. Dyslexic brains struggle to connect information because of where the information gets filed, owing to the pathways and routes it takes. This is not the fault of either the brain or the person, but is simply how a brain is wired to receive information. It is our job as teachers and parents to support pupils in developing strategies and skills to navigate themselves through the difficulties that their wiring creates.

I felt sick, yet excited at the same time, because I realised that second brain was mine. That crazy, disorganised, Mary Poppins bag brain is my actual brain! When I write essays, I struggle to link information together, to see how it connects, and to know where I have stored it.

There were more revelations for me over the next

four days. One of these was about working memory. I learned that our memory has many functions and parts: visual memory allows us to learn by seeing, auditory memory allows us to learn by hearing and long-term memory holds on to all the facts, experiences and knowledge we have. And then, there is working memory.

Working memory is the part of our brain that does all the work. It must cope under pressure and we use it all the time to process visual and auditory information. It does exactly what it describes, working to filter, understand and file away new information. For dyslexic people, this is often an area of significant weakness and the area which is the biggest hindrance to making academic progress and coping with everyday life. In the same way that we are not in control of how our brains are wired, we are also not in control of how large our working memory space is. Once it is full, it needs emptying, and if we only have a small working memory space it is going to need emptying far more often. This process is hard work and exhausting and this may explain why I just can't keep up in lecture environments!

If someone has a deficit in working memory, the chances are that their memory is very easily overloaded. It's no wonder that dyslexic children in class often become unmotivated and switch off.

Working memory difficulties can impact us in several ways, often first showing when someone is learning to read. As an example, when sounding the word 'cat' imagine you are an alien and this is an unknown word to you. As you approach the word you must remember the first letter and what it sounds like. You then sound it out and move to the next, you begin the process again. What does it look like? What letter is it? What sound does it make? You then sound it out and move on to the last letter. Again, what letter is it? What's the sound? Now blend them all back together again and relate it to a word that you know!

If you have a deficit in working memory, the chances are your memory would have become overloaded halfway through reading the letter 'a'. These issues are further compounded if you have difficulties in visual processing, recognising the sounds quickly or remembering the sound that the letter represents. This is a worst-case scenario, but it gives you an idea of how hard a brain with specific learning difficulties has to work just to learn the basics of reading.

In addition, if you are using all your working memory capacity to break down and blend words back together, how on earth are you supposed to understand what you are reading? This was my issue. While I had a good visual memory, I had learnt to read lots of words by sight, without sounding them out. Once words had more than two syllables or had complex consonant or vowel patterns, I had to work really, really hard to sound them out. This is why I have to read things several times.

I learned about a method called Direct Discovery Teaching, which enables the learner to discover for themselves how information links together. It builds on existing knowledge, finding the existing bit of information in the brain and glues new information on top. Direct Discovery Teaching is a way of helping to file the information we receive, constantly reinforcing the pathway to make it easier to retrieve. Without realising it, this is what I had previously done with my set of low attaining children.

Understanding and learning about metacognition was one of the most useful skills I learnt over these four days. Put simply, metacognition is thinking about thinking. Thinking about what we know, to work out what we do not know, and building on existing knowledge. It is a hugely powerful tool to any learner, especially a dyslexic one. A skilled specialist teacher will be the facilitator in children's learning, not spoon feeding them but instead leading the way with gentle prompts and precision planning that allows mistakes to be made. The most important are the mistakes discovered by the learner themselves. This approach is not as damaging to self-esteem, because it builds on existing knowledge, making success far more possible.

Another huge piece of learning for me was open and closed syllables, and I use this all the time now as a strategy myself. To understand open and closed syllables you need to know the vowels, the consonants and the difference between the long and short vowel sounds. For example, robot has an open and a closed syllable 'rO- bot'. The first 'o' makes the long sound as there is no consonant at the end of the first syllable. The second syllable makes the short 'o' sound because it is closed in by a consonant. Suddenly, I was reminded again of teaching my low attaining set. We had spent ages developing the knowledge of counting syllables in words and learning the long and short vowel sounds.

After four days of revelations, new learning, and a number of moments where I felt out of my depth, I left London on a high. Not only did I know I would succeed on the course, it set me thinking: if I have learnt all this in four days, how much could I learn in a year?

In my heart, I knew I was probably dyslexic, but didn't feel the need to get assessed immediately, because I thought back to many of the pupils I had worked with and suddenly could easily think of at least twenty that probably had undiagnosed dyslexia.

I felt guilty for not understanding or truly knowing how it felt for them, and I felt like I had failed them in some way.

There were children who had been so verbally articulate in class, who used amazing vocabulary when talking and during discussions, but never seemed able to get their ideas down on paper.

Equally, there had been pupils who were completely unable to build any sort of sight vocabulary, who knew all the right letters but who muddled them when spelling. Other pupils often mixed sounds when they were talking, for example saying 'par cark' instead of 'car park'!

Then there were the pupils who never seemed to produce anything other than a few lines of work, but the work they did produce was beautiful and perfect! Suddenly the amount of effort they would have had to put into that work became evident to me. I felt dreadful for all the times I had told these pupils to hurry up and work faster! In my mind, I could also see a group of children like me. They were well-behaved but quiet, working hard, just getting on with it, hoping no-one noticed they had not really understood. I knew how soul-destroying it was to have work that looked like you had only done enough to get by, when, in fact, the effort you had placed into the work had been mammoth. It was unseen, and so went unacknowledged.

More importantly, there was something closer to home to worry about. My son had started school, and he didn't seem to be learning as quickly as I thought he would. Many of the things I had learnt on the course could apply to him. I needed to forget about myself for a moment, turning my focus, energy and attention to him.

HISTORY REPEATING ITSELF

My son had started preschool aged two-and-a-half, and at the age of four, when the cards designed to begin to introduce letters and sounds started to come home, he was simply not interested. He was still far too busy, doing important digging in the mud, working out how things went together (and came apart), building road and train tracks, and discussing daily events. When I did manage to get him to sit down and do them, the results were inconsistent. Letters he would know and be secure with one day, appeared to just fall out of his head the next day. There was no pattern, no rhyme or reason to which ones he knew and which ones he didn't. There was no confusion over his b's and his d's, just inconsistency across the board.

On starting school this same pattern continued, and when reading books came home it was a battle to get him to look at them. He knew all the letter sounds in isolation, but did not seem to get the concept that they could be blended together to make whole words. The teacher would send a few books home every week, but I had to ask her to slow down. She was overwhelming him, and I could see he was just not ready to move on to the next book. He was still having to break every single word down, was not gaining any sight vocabulary and the phonic approach was clearly incredibly hard work for him.

The books the school used at the time were phonic-based books, simply made up of words using the sounds he had learnt. This meant they were words like 'nit', 'sip', and 'nat', all words which we don't often come across. He had to sound every single word out, which made reading a chore rather than something he could enjoy. To sit for ten minutes, and in that time sound out only ten words is painful not only for the person reading but also the person listening!

I knew my son was clever, but I couldn't see why he wasn't able to learn to read quickly and efficiently. His language was phenomenal for a four-year-old, and always had been advanced. He had developed vocabulary quickly as a toddler. At just twenty-one months, just as he became a brother, the health visitor was astounded at how well developed his language was. So, given how bright and articulate he appeared, why was he not reading? Elsewhere, his maths was ticking along and he seemed to be acquiring basic number facts, but ultimately his reading was the real stumbling block for him. Alongside this he hated writing, and with very poor pencil control he could still barely write his name.

I became a pushy mum as he entered the next academic year, although the teachers didn't really know this because I found ways of doing it so quietly, trying to keep discussions under the radar and off the record. Despite sustained and significant effort from the school, their approach and systems weren't working for him. I decided I had the skills to teach him to read, having taught everyone else's children, so now I would teach him!

I used a set of books published by Pearson called 'Rapid Readers'. It is these books which are responsible for my son learning to read, with a lot of time spent working through them with me, but most importantly and undoubtedly his new-found skills were the result of tonnes of hard graft, grit and determination from him. Every night, my husband would bath our daughter while my son and I would spend half an hour reading through the books, completing the worksheets and doing timed reading activities.

Timed reading activities are when five words are

repeated on a grid at random several times. The pupil reads them as fast as they can while they are being timed. The idea is that with each attempt they try to beat their own best time. It provides opportunities for overlearning, and is a way of seeing each word hundreds of times so that it can be secured in the long-term memory. By learning some words in this way and having them transferred to long-term memory, it helps to free up some working memory space to work out the other words around them.

Rapid books were great for my son because his language and vocabulary ability were good. The words within these books were words he knew; although they were not necessarily words he could read, they were words he used often in everyday conversation. While a confident reader can simply read the tricky words, he would often guess the tricky words. He would often guess correctly, by being able to fall back on his incredible understanding of language and vocabulary. For example, he could not read the word 'rocket' in isolation, but when reading a book about the moon, the sentence 'Blast went the rocket' was easy for him to work out by using all these skills. I didn't teach him to read, he did that himself. I just gave him the time and showed him the skills he needed to be able to do it!

His other problem was writing. He hated writing. Not only is he a boy, but also is a May baby. There has been, and continues to be, lots of research undertaken showing that boys born in the summer months are more likely to make slower progress, and not perform as well academically as those born in other seasons.

He didn't see the point of committing pen to paper when he could talk so much more fluidly about a subject instead. He had never been interested in sitting and drawing, and his pencil control and handwriting were still very poor. He struggled to form the letters correctly, often unable to remember how to start a letter, but also found it difficult to spell the words once he had the letters formulated. More importantly, he struggled to remember what he originally set out to say because his working memory was so overloaded.

While he stumbled and tripped his way through his school work, the curriculum continued to crank up over time, however, his spirit never faltered and he always tried his best. Both his teachers and teaching assistants thought he was marvellous and, recognising his vibrant spirit, cast him in the leading role as Santa Claus in the school's Christmas play.

When his summer report came home, the extent to which he was behind was now very apparent and panic began to set in for me. I remember asking his class teacher if I needed to be more concerned about his progress, wondering if perhaps he had something going on that I needed to sort out. Until this point, I had not put any pressure on my son, we had done the extra work on his reading skills, but that is a life skill he desperately needed to have in place to support the rest of his education. At no point had I made him do writing or extra work at home, knowing how much he hated it. The teacher reassured me that he would get there, just at his own pace.

It wasn't long after this I spotted the next sign that he was potentially dyslexic. He had loved going to school, skipping in everyday, oblivious that he just wasn't getting out of it what he needed. Suddenly, and almost overnight, he realised that he was behind, and quite quickly he realised that a major weakness was his writing. I think perhaps at this point the staff at the school hadn't fully understood my concerns were genuine considering my professional perspective, and I think they thought I was simply a pushy mother wanting him to be something he wasn't. This, however, was not the case.

I knew he was bright, but I also knew that there was something holding him back. It could have been motherly instinct, I guess, but I also had the skills from my professional life backing me, and my professional knowledge led me to consider the concept that dyslexia can be hereditary. Since I suspected that my dad, grandad and myself were all dyslexic, there was a high possibility that my son could be too. Luckily an amazing Higher Level Teaching Assistant, who specialised in SEND helped him.

She carried out a few assessments with him exploring his non-verbal and verbal ability, and while these were not in-depth assessments, they were standardised tests that would provide an indication of his underlying ability. He blew us all away, attaining high scores in both areas. This was not a child who should be low attaining, but a bright child experiencing a specific learning difficulty, who was desperately under achieving as a result of it. I had to find a way to remove the barriers.

The trouble was, as I had done before him, he was beginning to hide the issues. He became the class clown, developing his own defence mechanism to talk his way out of work. He was spending large amounts of the school day in a group outside the classroom with the teaching assistant which, although done with the best of intentions, was so damaging to him it would take several years for him to get over it. I want to make it clear the teaching assistant was lovely; he loved her and he also loved his teacher. The damaging part was the message that sending him out of the classroom subconsciously gave him.

His perception of this entire situation still haunts me, and I still wish I could have fixed it for him. I did try, as did his dad, but it was already too far out of our control. I remember holding his hand as we walked home from school one day and asking him about his day. He asked me what he had done to upset his teacher? I said that I did not understand what he meant. He went on to explain: 'Well Mummy, I am not allowed to stay in the classroom and do my learning. I have to go out with my helper and a small group. They mess about Mummy and I can't get anything done. I don't know what I have done to make my teacher sad with me.' He was just five years old.

What is so sad is I know that his teacher had the absolute best intentions at heart, genuinely believing that this small group was the right course and that it would support him, enabling him to learn at a pace appropriate to him and so make better progress. Instead, it only served to force him into hiding; pushing him into a comfort zone that he did not want to be in. He wanted to be seen, to be noticed, and to learn. Instead at the age of just five, he perceived himself as having done something wrong. He was trying his hardest but, since his hardest was not good enough, he felt he was being punished by not being allowed in the classroom.

I had conversations with his teacher, but the teacher felt strongly that this was the only way forward for him. At the time, I was not in a position to argue. Instead, I just had to watch the life slowly be sucked out of him, as his confidence and self-esteem dipped further and further into the gutter. I did for him whatever I could at home but, in reality, it was only damage limitation.

What made it worse was that he had a sister who was like a sponge, picking everything up so quickly, and I knew he could see the gap between them closing in. His smile and the exuberance he once had in his school life were dwindling; his feet were beginning to drag, and you could see school becoming more effort for him as time passed. For now, all I could do was support his needs as I tried to balance them with mine. Life was becoming increasingly challenging as I juggled my own personal needs with both my work life and my own family's needs. We were all walking on an icy tightrope and, fearing we could slip off at any time, I knew something needed to change, but I couldn't work out what.

Thankfully, my friendship with Unbiological helped keep me on the tightrope, and the more we got to know each other, Unbiological started to see right through my charade, just as The Trumpet Player and Five Minutes Fast had done before her. She approached it differently though: whilst she never directly acknowledged that my insecurities were there, she gently challenged me in ways I did not know I could be challenged.

I still felt inferior to her, but we now had conversations about education and parenting in which I felt like I was her equal. I soaked up her company, which was addictive. She made me feel good about myself, and I began to feel that suddenly I had an opinion that was actually valued. However, there was no hiding with her - she saw right through me and, like a sly, old fox, she prized me out from the safety of my cover.

She began to show me that there was another way, smoking me out of the cold ground I had sought refuge in for so long. Slowly, but surely, I no longer felt the need to hide.

For the first time, I wanted to be seen, and be noticed. I wanted to feel alive; to confront my fears, weaknesses and failures. I no longer wanted to be invisible. She revolutionised my life, and helped me find a new beginning.

SPRING

Courage:

"To be brave when you feel scared, walking directly into danger and confronting it head on to seek resolution."

(Jo Rees, 2017)

BATTLING CHANGE

The daffodils line the pavements, moving their heads towards the warming sun as it burns through the frost in the morning. It leaves behind dewy puddles and grass that glitters, fresh and green. Buds shoot from the trees and from the rose bushes, as I walk heavily pregnant towards school and nursery. The air is fresh and clean – the smell of hope and fresh starts.

Baby number three is now overdue. I am exhausted, working late in the previous night desperately trying to complete an assignment for the dyslexia diploma. It has been hard, but I am so glad I started it straight after the Postgraduate Certificate. I am hoping I will be able to complete the second half once the baby arrives. Once I have the diploma, I will be able to competently assess and diagnose dyslexia.

I have often wondered over the preceding weeks how much easier it might be if I had been given extra time to complete my assignments. I wonder if I would meet the criteria. I know that I need to get an official diagnosis of dyslexia for myself, but I feel scared at what an Educational Psychologist may find.

What if they find that I am not, in fact, dyslexic, but just stupid? My mind then flits to the possibility of redundancy at work. I'm not even sure I will have a job to go back to after this baby. Maternity leave has shielded me for a few months from the threat of a restructuring, but the imminent danger of the elimination of my service hangs over my head.

The March breeze on my face reddens my cheeks, giving me a healthy glow. My mind flits back to the baby as it gently kicks to remind me it is there. For the hundredth time, I go through my birth plan in my head, determined once again to take control in this birth, and not let anyone else tell me how I am going to deliver this baby. Nature will take its course, I will listen to my body and I won't let anyone distract me from the natural rhythm or emotions I feel. From somewhere I have found a confidence from deep within and, just as bulbs will surely break through the ground to reach the sun, inevitably some bulbs may never flower owing to the shade. I am in control, however, and will make sure I am seen and heard, and that I get what I need.

I arrive in the delivery room, and immediately demand pethidine. I tell them I have no intention of sitting on the bed at any time and I will be standing. The midwife wants to get a monitor on me to check the baby's heartbeat. 'Fine,' I reply, 'as long as you can do it with me standing up.' They oblige, but, unable to reliably monitor my unborn baby, I am made to sit on the bed. Although I have no intention of being off my feet for long, with the monitor on all I can hear is the baby's erratically dipping heartbeat. With my anxiousness growing, and the memories of my previous labours now feeling increasingly raw, it was decided that it might be time to call in a doctor to intervene. Instead, I decide it is time for me to push.

Ten minutes later, I have been handed a beautiful baby girl who now lays delicately in my arms. I have done it again, on my own, but more importantly, I have done it at my own pace. I have been in control. This time I have not let myself be intimidated by the knowledge of others. I trusted my maternal instincts, seeing them as equal, and perhaps even superior, to their medical knowledge.

I return home the following day with my bundle of joy, and during that first night back at home the clocks roll forward an hour, marking the impending approach of warmer weather. Instead of all the positivity and renewed purpose I knew I should now be feeling, a strange sense of foreboding now surrounds me; like the wind of change, I just feel different.

The lighter evenings now expose the beauty of spring as I walk through the streets, pushing the pram on an evening stroll. A million things fly around my head. I reflect on the day; having three children under five; all the preparation for each day, list keeping, date remembering, appointment making, daily chores, plus juggling a job and a husband. It is becoming increasingly difficult to keep on top of all this, and I know that I am struggling to keep myself a step ahead of everything.

I am exhausted and sustaining a smile is becoming harder. It is increasingly difficult to hide away from the world. However, I can't be invisible, because I have three children who keep me very much visible to the wider world. We are being invited places to play, to parties, and parents' evenings. There always seems to be someone in the house, always someone around. It means that I have less and less opportunity to let my guard down, which means I must sustain the act for longer, with more pretending, which in turn is more and more exhausting. Everything begins to take its toll, and I physically hurt inside holding it all in. There are times when I feel like I might burst, but I know that if I do crack, the dam will open and I won't be able to hold it back.

By now, Unbiological's husband ('Mr. Unbiological') has also seen through to the real me. At dinner one night with mutual friends of ours, it began to bother me how he continued to notice me despite my trying to hide in the shadows. He actively kept me involved in the discussions, showing no fear of exposing the cracks I was still trying so hard to hide. I know, deep down, why his opinions matter so much to me; it's because he reminds me so much of my Dad's dad. I always listen to him, and to this day I still instinctively seek out his approval and reassurance, just as I once did from my grandad. It's actually really comforting, and perhaps in some small way, helps fill part of the hole my grandad left in my heart when he passed away.

On the surface, Mr. Unbiological has the same loveable arrogance and intolerant nature that my grandad did: loud, brash, and indestructible. He is also possibly one of the most impatient people I know! I realise that I must drive him mad with some of the things I say, and I know that he must also wonder why on earth I have just said what I have, however, he never says it aloud; instead I sense a reassuring vibe radiating from him: 'You are better than that!'

Deep down, he has a soft spot for me, and, while

he has seen straight through my façade, unlike everyone else he is not prepared to play along with my game, and avoid exposing the issues I am trying to conceal. He openly challenges me, and doesn't tolerate my attempts at hiding.

While this scares me, leaving me feeling small, and sometimes even uneasy, at the same time it also drives me towards a belief in myself. I know I have a soft spot for him though, because I can see straight through him as well. I am sure that he too is dyslexic.

He keeps himself distanced from most people and the arrogant and intolerant shield he has built to protect himself is his defence, just as mine is my smile. His greatest weapon and strength is this resilient self-built wall. Behind the wall, which he rarely lets down, is the insecure, caring, sensitive, and intuitive person he really is. Not many people see this in him, and cannot see past the wall. I do, in fact it is all I see, and I am not fooled. I don't let him pretend with me. We are one and the same; we each have our own weapons and defences but they have been created for the same reasons.

Behind his wall, he is as broken as I am.

Feeling broken inside, I continue to push myself hard, getting the children in bed by seven so that I can study every night until eleven. I know I am beginning to fall apart, but I try hard to keep myself behind an icy screen and hope the summer sun doesn't come too quickly and melt it away.

My back hurts all the time and I head to the

chiropractor where I notice a business card for a counsellor who specialises in weight management, building confidence and self-esteem. I feel massive and hate my post-pregnancy body, but I've no idea if I am brave enough to go and see her.

A few weeks pass and I finally pluck up enough courage to make an appointment. Week after week, I revisit and it turns out to be one of the most exhilarating and cathartic things I have done in my life so far. I don't want to fake it anymore and am too tired to keep on pretending. My smile is fake and it hurts to use it. I want to be the best mum I can be for my children, but living in a constant battle of staying ahead of the game is not allowing that to happen.

I continue to plough away at the diploma, slowly but surely moving in the right direction. Like a sunflower growing or a ripening strawberry, you hardly notice the gradual change until you think back to what it looked like a week ago, and realise how far it has come in that time, but you can't pinpoint a specific time at when it physically changed.

The email pings through informing me I have failed my module on assessments, although strangely it doesn't affect my self-esteem. In fact, I am not worried as I submitted this particular assignment early. At the time, I was criticised by my tutor for rushing it, but this was an intentional ploy and strategy, since this module relied heavily on reading the manuals that come with the assessments. Having read the manuals as best as I could several times over until my eyes ached and my brain hurt, I knew that I had not fully understood them. Since I knew from previous assignments that my tutor gave very thorough feedback, I knew that if what I submitted wasn't good enough, she would talk me through each stage on the telephone. I would also receive written feedback.

Learning from mistakes is still my best strategy. While mistakes can be damaging to self-esteem if we are caught off guard, when they are made in a controlled, supported environment or when we are in direct control of them, mistakes are the most powerful tools we own, and should be used to our advantage. I am 100% in control of this error, having submitted the assignment early, because I had learned all I could on my own. I was using metacognition to help me succeed. I had my starting point in place, and just needed to be nurtured back on track and in the right direction, which I now had by way of the feedback.

A wisteria cannot show its natural beauty unless it is encouraged to entwine its new shoots on a trellis, but once guided, the beautiful purple flowers will hang delicately, but definitely, hiding the scarred brown branches and allowing only its beauty to be judged.

Taking the feedback and building on it, I confidently hit the resubmit button for the final time on the rewritten assignment. I feel sure I will pass this time, and look over to my chuckling baby girl who fills my heart with joy and makes the effort worthwhile.

Today, a letter came through the door. I had passed. I have earned my diploma in dyslexia. I should be proud, but instead I feel only exhaustion. I feel like I have climbed a mountain, with no map to get back down.

As I stand in my kitchen reading the letter, I am covered in cake mix and butter cream icing, as is the rest of the kitchen. One hundred and twenty perfectly iced cupcakes with individually crafted fondant Lego bricks on top grace the sideboard. The stand that the cakes will be presented on, made from Duplo Lego bricks, sits in a box next to them. It is the hottest day of the year, and I have spent it in the kitchen making cakes for Mr. Unbiological's fortieth birthday! This evening I will relax with many of my friends and quietly reap the reward I have sown. However, tonight I won't mention that I passed my diploma, as I have not made them aware I had even been studying for it. If they congratulated me, I'd be embarrassed, not knowing what to say. Instead I will be noticed for the cakes - the care and attention I put into each one is obvious. It is my way of showing platonic love for the people who have unknowingly helped me and spurred me on without realising or knowing who I really am.

My husband silently looks and smiles at me as he walks into the kitchen and starts to clear up the carnage in the wake of my cupcake creations! Effortlessly and quietly he stands beside me. Without saying a word, he runs hot water and begins to wash up. His unconditional love protects me and never lets me down. Together we keep moving forward. Sometimes in sunshine, sometimes in rain, and sometimes in cloud. Never does it feel cold and never do the seasons stay the same.

BELIEVE IN YOURSELF

I ran the dyslexic provision for my Local Authority for three and a half years. It ended in redundancy, because the council didn't feel the service was value for money. As you can imagine I fought, just as fiercely as I had fought for most of the things I believe in. I battled to change and adapt the service, but my voice was too small against those who were against me. I felt they had superior intelligence, years more service, and, ultimately, wielded far more power than I did. One person, in particular, was good at manipulating facts and data to her advantage. Initially, I allowed this to get to me, but when I realised this was a battle I was never going to win, I exerted my energy in another direction. Again, it's not about giving up; it's about knowing when you can't make a difference on your own and when you have to pick a different battle.

By now, I had established that I needed to change

my thinking about myself. My ongoing counselling was helping me to discover my confidence, but also to speak my mind, stand up tall and be brave. It wasn't a crime to think something different from the person next to you, and it was ok to be wrong. I was learning that whilst my ideas were not always rooted in the theory, I often spoke sense and I had strong and sensible ideas.

While I had not yet had a formal diagnosis, I knew now in my heart of hearts I was dyslexic. This was an enormous strength and comfort to me. The fact that I found things difficult was not my fault; it was nothing I had done wrong, but most importantly, I was realising it was not that I wasn't listening hard enough, not that I wasn't working hard enough and it was not because I was stupid.

I had begun to accept that I most likely had a difficulty that I wasn't in control of. Now I had enough knowledge through my own learning to begin to overcome it. Years and years of living on the edge had brought me to this point. I just wasn't happy accepting that I wasn't in control. My need to learn constantly had got me this far through life. I knew this drive to learn would get me through this.

My silent inner strength was my secret power. I had got through so much without realising it that my resilience was second nature, yet this was a weapon I had not even realised I had developed. I refer to it as a weapon because, to me, that's what resilience is. It is my weapon I use in conjunction with my smile to protect myself and to survive.

While I still had lots of weaknesses, to many people they continued to be hidden from view behind a smile. My smile was my defence, and while it could be cracked, it would and could not be broken indefinitely.

The service I worked for was about to be disbanded. From the ashes of the service a phoenix was growing. I knew by now I was worth something and that I had valuable skills. I had a reputation for working with SEN children and their families, and I was well respected by my colleagues. I needed to use all these assets to my advantage.

I applied for a part-time job working across three schools, a position for which there were several candidates and competition was fierce. One of the interview panel told me afterwards that my sheer passion and enthusiasm for wanting to work with people who have additional needs and make a difference to their lives radiated from me. She told me that this passion oozed from me as I spoke to them, and the interview panel had hung on my every word. I was clearly dedicated, loyal, and loved my work. This person was right. I loved the idea of the new job; I loved that I would be able to make a difference and I could still undertake my own personal mission to change the world, even just one child or family at a time! I started the job that September, contracted for two days a week.

So often in life things don't turn out as planned. This job was exactly that. I started thinking it was going to take me in a very specific direction, however, it ended up taking me in a completely different and unexpected one, ending in a way I could never even have imagined at the outset. Who would have thought that a workplace or job could be capable of breaking a heart? For now, I was content and happy, knowing I had a new job to conquer, and that everything was continuing to go in the direction that I wanted it to.

However, I hadn't realised I had yet to truly come to terms with my diagnosis, and that this would prove the hardest battle I was going to have to fight.

PURGATORY

Very shortly after being appointed, I ended up working in just one school rather than across three, as was originally planned. This didn't matter to me. There was so much to do in this school, and I had so many ideas. I knew that I could make a difference. After a year of finding my feet, I was firmly a member of what was an amazing staff team. There was something special about the team at this time, and I will never forget the feeling of belonging I had initially in this job. I felt like it was exactly where I needed to be, safe and secure. For someone who had had issues with seeing herself as a valuable person, having spent years keeping myself as inconspicuous as possible, this was a revolutionary concept I had begun to accept. For the first time, I wanted to be seen and I wanted to be needed. It was a revelation to my mind.

My counselling sessions had now finished, having been the most amazing journey unlocking grief and anger I had no idea I was holding on to. I had confronted so many insecurities: the relationships with my own children, my feelings of not being valued, my resentment at having to grow up at eight years old, my confidence, my self-esteem, my eating, my weight, friendships at school, and all the things I had kept hidden. One by one they had been eliminated. I had hidden them because I was too ashamed to ask for help, thinking I was worthless, all because I had not understood the simplest of tasks. I didn't want people to know how stupid I really was so I covered it up, hoping that no-one would notice, but only served to hurt myself in doing do.

All my difficulties stemmed from the same root. Like a stubborn dandelion root which has buried itself deep in the ground, it needed to be pulled out. All my feelings revolved around my ridiculously low self-esteem, rock-bottom self-belief, feelings of worthlessness, inequality and invisibility. At this point I felt sure this had stemmed from years of feeling stupid and feeling like I couldn't do simple things well. Instead, I felt like an underdog, and so often out of my depth. These things were in fact all symptoms of undiagnosed dyslexia.

A diagnosis suddenly became important; it would provide the answers I needed to bring closure to my past and finally enable me to become the person I now realised I was capable of being. I wasn't looking for an excuse, but instead wanted to begin to understand my past and make sense of it. In doing so, it would help me plan and live my future.

I approached a private educational psychologist, 'The Smile', who was a colleague. She was mortified when I asked her to assess me! She could not believe I was even considering it. 'How can you possibly be dyslexic? You are amazing at your job! Are you really sure?' she said.

'Yes,' I confirmed. In my mind, I was silently begging her not to offer me any opportunity to change my mind and back out. I needed to know. Ironically, I arrived for this assessment on the wrong evening. I was a day early. You would have thought that by now that I would, by default, write everything down to avoid these mix-ups, particularly where dates are concerned. Even after years of just getting by in life, I continue to have to retrain myself.

Once again, the following evening, I arrive at The Smile's house. I know that she is still unconvinced at this point that the assessment was going to unearth any issues, nevertheless she appeases me, and the assessment begins.

My confidence really grew, and I started to find my voice and use it in a more controlled way over the following years. I had gradually become fulltime in my job and I felt I was really making a positive difference in people's lives. I was good at what I did, and most of the time I believed it too. So many staff at my school touched, changed and shaped me.

In the beginning, the light was so bright. I was surrounded by inspirational people who loved to teach and were all fantastic at it. Whether they were leaders, teachers, admin staff, or teaching assistants, we were all united in our common purpose: to support and change the lives of people.

Amongst the glow of light, I found my 'Work Mum' and 'Fellow Smiler'. I had known the lady I refer to as 'Work Mum' for over ten years, our paths having regularly crossed at various meetings, conferences and courses. By some strange coincidence, or maybe even fate, she ended up working at the desk next to me. 'Fellow Smiler' had been a long-time school friend whose path had crossed mine many times, but it was here at this place and time we realised how strong we both were.

I now had my official diagnosis of dyslexia, and this really helped me. It was not an excuse, but it enabled me to approach things differently. If I was handed the pen on a course, I gave it a go, without the same feeling of panic I'd felt so often before. I simply said, 'You will have to excuse my spelling, I find spelling hard.'

This did not mean I was stupid or my opinions counted less, it meant that I needed to use a dictionary or spellchecker, or ask for help. I bumbled through each day, and the time seemed to just fly. However, I could feel it was coming again - that feeling of being too comfortable; the feeling of not learning anything new. Ironically, this same comfortable feeling made me feel completely uncomfortable. I knew that I needed to push myself forward, but everything seemed against me.

I was slowly changing my mind-set to focus on the positives. This was enabling me to not only find these positives, but to realise that I possessed the most amazing collection of special gifts.

Why had I not seen this earlier? There was so much light shining. I LOVED this job, I loved my colleagues, and I loved the families and children I worked with. In return, I gave it everything, and often found myself prioritising my job above my own needs and family.

I wonder now in hindsight, if there was too much light and if I was perhaps blinded and maybe didn't see the flaws, because suddenly and unexpectedly, almost overnight, everything changed. To this day, I still do not know why. I did know why I no longer felt safe, secure, and happy at a place that had, until then, offered these things in abundance. I suddenly realised that this was NOT where I needed to be. I questioned whether perhaps they didn't need me anymore; perhaps my work here was done. Being good at my job was what I had been using to define me, but my expectations were now so high, the only way would be… could be… down.

Things changed for me personally too, as we experienced a tragic and unexpected loss in our family. Someone who was not much older than me. I had to face it head on. I was a grown up now. Not only that, but I was the grown up that had to deal with it. I was the grown up that took control and the grown up who held it all together.

In the midst of all this, I finally realised how my family viewed me. I never quite felt a part of my family, because I didn't ever let them see the real me. For the first time, I let them see the real me. I cried, and I said exactly what I was thinking, even when it was difficult to say or hear. I exposed my vulnerability, but I also exposed my strength, courage, and honesty. At the same time, I discovered how strong I was, and how much I could take, exceeding limits I did not even know existed.

I have always known I am lucky to be part of such a tight-knit extended family, but I honestly don't think I appreciated the strength and power we had between us until this time. This death changed the relationship between me, my sister and my cousins forever. The bond between us was always unbreakable, but I didn't know how much I loved and needed them until this time. I'd not realised how much they had been a massive part of shaping me and keeping me safe when I was on my own path of self-destruction in the years gone by.

We will never call each other cousins again. We are sisters, forged at the darkest and most desperate of times, feeling each other's pain as if it were our own. It is a cliché, but it is true, in that you should never underestimate the power of love. Love for my family during this time was like an unstoppable magic potion that engulfed us in an invisible blanket we all shared.

Our greatest weapon. Our greatest shield. Our love for each other is indestructible.

A few weeks after the loss, as life inevitably began to seep back in, the feelings of insecurity came flooding back. I wanted to be invisible, but I also wanted to have a voice. I wanted to be needed, but at the same time to go unnoticed. There was a complete contradiction of emotions and feelings that made no sense to me at all. I kept going, because that's what resilient people do, and that's what I do. You don't stop. You never ever stop. You just push yourself forward. One foot in front of the other.

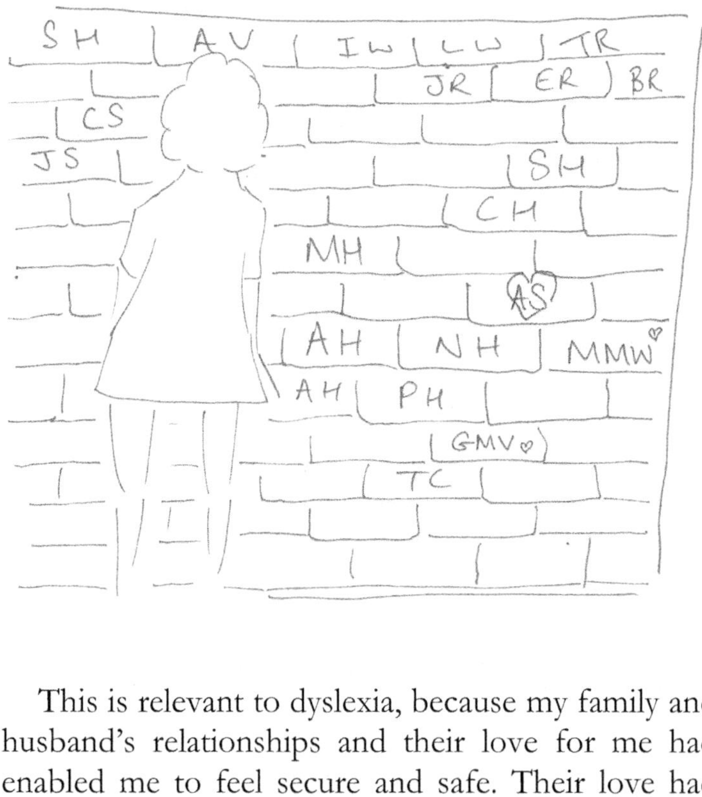

This is relevant to dyslexia, because my family and husband's relationships and their love for me had enabled me to feel secure and safe. Their love had enabled me to keep my insecurities hidden. The huge protection they had provided had kept me on a positive path. Without them this is not where I would have been.

I tried to change things at work, applying for other jobs. I had several interviews for new jobs. I got through the first day of one, but was not invited back for the second day. The feedback I was given was that the panel felt I was not resilient enough to hold a senior role. Perhaps they were right, maybe I wasn't resilient, maybe I was just kidding myself.

I did not get shortlisted for a couple of other jobs I applied for, and the resilient comment haunted me. I dwelt on it for a while, unable to get it out of my head.

I think it got to me because I know I am really resilient to have achieved all that I have. It felt so personal because they did not know resilience was my weapon of choice, and that my resilience was currently all that was keeping me from drowning in an ongoing ocean of grief, insecurities and feelings of unworthiness. Eventually, I rationalised it, deciding that the comment on my resilience was a cop out excuse. How can you make a judgement on someone's resilience when you have only known them for a day? I had been taken on face value, my smile masking the true depth of me, hiding the complex understanding, knowledge, and talents that I held.

Still I plodded on, but found myself smiling less and less. I desperately tried to seek out new challenges in my current position, convincing myself to be satisfied with all that I had. Everyday felt so full of negativity. The more I tried to change things, the more difficult they became. I knew I was bringing myself down with my thoughts. Work Mum said to me one day, 'Thoughts are like buses - we can choose whether we get on them or let them go past.'

She was right and I knew what she was saying, but it seemed like the negative buses came past more frequently and were far more noticeable.

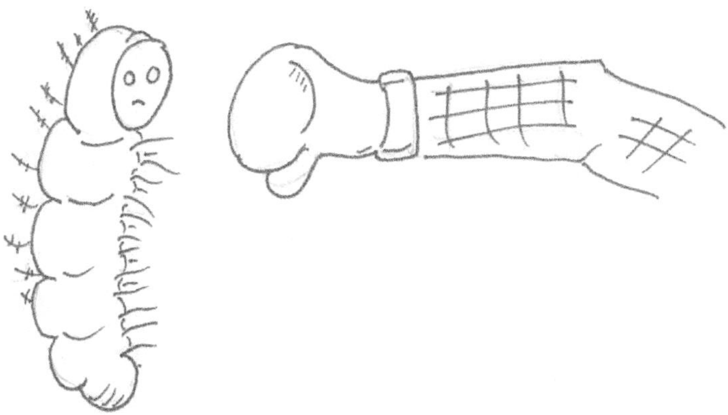

A series of unusual events happened to me at work, knocking me as I had never been knocked before. It turned out that support from my school was not how I had imagined it might be at a time of crisis, such as the one I was now experiencing. The school had got bigger, and the light was becoming fragmented and inconsistent, not only for me, but for all of us, I think. Situations kept presenting themselves, and unintentionally I always seemed to be involved in drama, despite all the right intentions.

Ironically, while doing the right thing for everyone else and executing it in an exemplary fashion, I was doing myself no favours. The pinnacle of bittersweet success.

I kept going. This was not about not having resilience; this was now about being too resilient, and I was just going to kept going regardless. Giving in or giving up were not options for me, and were not options I ever considered. I just repeated the words under my breath 'Must work harder, must keep going, must try harder to impress and be noticed.' The words that were my mantra to life.

Suddenly, I was back to the default setting I had developed in those A-level English lessons years ago. Giving 110% and no-one noticing or acknowledging how hard I was working, or how much I was hurting. This is a sad and desolate place to be, especially when you are so passionate and desperate to please. I so wanted to make a positive difference, but all my actions were not getting me anywhere. More often than not, the only movement ended up being in a direction I didn't anticipate going.

Eventually, an event at work brought me to a point where I felt unable to continue. It was an event which had a catastrophic impact on me and my family, personally and professionally. I knew I had to stop and to take stock of where I was, but I was so scared that if I stopped I would never get going again.

I was falling, harder and faster than I had ever fallen before. Thirty-six years of cracks finally shattered. My smile completely disappeared and I was finally broken. I felt totally empty. All that remained for a few weeks was the shadow of a being that was once tenacious, bright and strong.

GRIEF

I have never felt as alone as I did in the following weeks.

I had taken up running as a means of managing my stress and anxiety. There was something both exhilarating and soothing about feeling the salty sea breeze rushing past my ears. It provided me with a sense of calm, and restored logical thinking.

When running one day, music blaring through my ears, I suddenly found myself able to make sense of so much of the past. I liked to live on the edge, I liked to be busy, it makes me feel alive. Dancing until it hurt, scratching my face until it bled, and pushing myself academically. It was the feeling of being uncomfortable that had driven me forward so many times.

I felt alone because the people who I most wanted

to notice me, didn't notice me at all. People who should have looked never once took the time to view things from my perspective. It felt like a test, not set by me but by the universe, designed to show me what really mattered in life. No-one stopped long enough to see how the impact from the event in my work life had, and continued to have, on me and my family.

Instead, my actions and responses were judged and criticised in an open forum. The years of cracks I had collected in my confidence and self-esteem, all stemming from the undiagnosed dyslexia, suddenly burst back open, and the crevices filled once again with the insecurities and past feelings of unworthiness. This was the final crack that broke me.

Well, I thought it had broken me. Deep down, however, something in me had changed.

In times gone by I would have let people bring me down. I worried too much about what people thought. In the past, I would have been quiet, embracing the chance to hide in the darkness, hoping that no one would find me. I wasn't prepared to do this anymore. I knew I deserved more than that. The incident involved me having to file a formal complaint, a process which involved managers at a much higher level than myself. I was still intimidated. They hadn't noticed me, so why would they want to listen to me? Initially, I didn't even try to get them to listen. I was just too broken, too fragile to even fight.

It was my son and my godson (Unbiological's son) that made me want to fight it. These two boys gave me hope.

My sensitive, emotionally literate, caring, philosophical and articulate son continued to find school difficult. He never got all his spellings right, his sisters were overtaking his reading ability, and he practised his times tables over and over but just didn't seem to be retaining them or getting any quicker at them. His trumpet was becoming more challenging because of the music theory now involved. His weapon of choice, on the surface, disengagement. Giving up before he had even tried. Baulking at the first hurdle and talking, talking in an attempt to get out of committing pen to paper! I was guilty and partly to blame.

I had lived in fear and did not want him to feel as I had done growing up. I did not want history to repeat itself - my dad, me and now him. I had kept him close, tried only to put him in the path of things where I knew he would be successful. This was, however, the fundamental flaw. How would he build resilience if he was never put in a situation where he needed to be resilient? I totally understood him, empathising with him on so many levels, but there was too much empathy.

When he said, 'I can't do it', I constantly told him he had to keep trying, to keep fighting and never, ever, give up. That said, he just did not have the skills he needed to keep going. In my attempt to keep him safe I had denied him of the opportunity to gain and develop the skills he needed to approach work or situations when they became tricky. I don't mean educational skills. I mean life skills. I mean the specific skill of resilience: the skill of making mistakes and learning from them in a safe environment. I knew I needed to change this.

Visiting Unbiological one evening, I discovered that my godson was struggling at high school. Unbiological asked me to talk to him, respecting my professional opinion. It turned out he was completely lacking in confidence owing to his dyslexia. I talked him through what his options were, guiding him through the situation. Not giving him answers, but showing him choices so he could see and make sense of them.

I got him, I get him. He was me twenty-six years ago.

He was in a place at the time that he too wanted

to be invisible. He talked to me crouched on the kitchen floor on the other side of the breakfast bar so that I couldn't see him. It was so painful to watch a bright, intelligent, and gifted young man want to disappear because he was not being provided with the correct support at school to help him overcome his dyslexic difficulties. It was even more personal because it was the same school that had let me down.

Part of growing up is living and surviving the tough stuff. Sadly, my son and godson, like all of us, will have to learn to fight their own battles in their own way. However, if they understand their own diagnosis better, it will help them understand themselves, which in turn will aid them in achieving their potential.

These two amazing individuals have special unique gifts they can offer the world, but were both losing sight of them, because their school constantly defined them by what they couldn't do or what they found difficult. I would not let them be defined by their weaknesses, but rather be defined by their gifts. I could not stand by and watch this happen.

I realised I didn't need to worry about my son or godson. The Unbiologicals and us, our families and close friends were all supporting our children in helping them to find and define their strengths.

This was my realisation: I couldn't do it on my own.

I had found my gifts through the love and support provided by my family and my closest friends. We needed to build a team around the boys, not to protect them, nor to do it for them, but to enable them to find their own strengths. This made me realise I needed to fight what had happened to me to make it right. I needed to fight it to show them that there was hope for people like us.

Sometimes in life things happen and everything changes, sometimes in an irreversible way. There was no going back, and the incident forced subsequent changes which had their own implications, the biggest of which was my decision to resign from my job.

The job I had once loved was no longer making me happy for many, many reasons. I felt that life was too short to be doing something that did not make me happy, or where I was not being challenged. My hard-working nature had been exploited, unintentionally I like to think, but whether it was intentional or not, this was undoubtedly how I felt. I felt personally and professionally let down by a place I had had so much respect and admiration for.

For a second time my heart was broken; it was a

different kind of pain, but nevertheless it hurt. The break was created by an unrequited love for my workplace. I was being pulled in a direction I did not want to go, but rather than going with it, I was fighting it, and fighting hard. However, I was fighting to go in the direction I knew I was destined to go.

My love affair with the place where I worked was over. I was dragging my heels, but I knew it was only a matter of time. I knew deep down, the people who mattered also knew it was over. My days had been numbered for a few months; it had just taken me a while to come to terms with it and to get to a place where I could accept it. I was finally brave enough and strong enough to walk away.

It took time to make peace with the events that happened which ultimately pushed me to my resignation. To me, it sadly felt like there was a clear and defined chain of events which led to this outcome. I was pushed, time and time again; poked and prodded; kicked whilst I was down. What made it more complicated was that no single person or situation was responsible for me feeling this way. The fact I genuinely cared for and loved the place so much was responsible for the emotions I now felt. This made it so much harder to come to terms with.

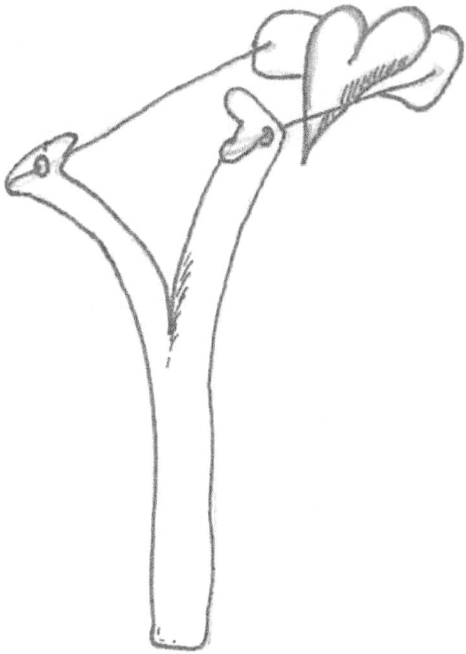

I wanted to be angry, scream, shout, and hate it. I just couldn't because, ultimately, while it was how I felt, perhaps I too was to blame. Perhaps I had created a situation which had to be managed and controlled. No-one asks to be placed on a pedestal and if I am saying that I am only human, the same is true of all people. No-one is perfect as perfection does not exist. It was my fault because I cared too much.

This was the hardest lesson I had learned in life so far. Just because you respect, trust and have faith in something this does not mean that you are valued in return. It does not mean that you are safe and can be protected unconditionally from events. At the end of the day, no-one owes you anything. My flaw and my fault.

I give my trust too freely, which might be considered naive at times. I know Unbiological, Five Minutes Fast and Scenic Route would all say I give too many chances. I am fiercely loyal, and dedicated to the point that no-one else could possibly match my unsurpassable dedication. I give more than I would ever expect in return, but I was finally done and I could finally see this was also a flaw.

Resignation was a defence mechanism to stop myself from any further hurt or disappointment. An attempt to protect myself from myself. It was my way of protecting my broken heart from my nature of giving 110% to everything, staying resilient, and keeping going at all costs. That workplace had had its pound of flesh and more besides, and I now had the scars to prove it. However, enough was enough.

I grieved for my job just as someone grieves for a person. The tears fell for weeks, and I just couldn't stop them. I felt all the other emotions that typically go hand-in-hand with grief: anger, hurt, depression, and anxiety. This toxic mix of feelings completely drained me, leaving me feeling empty. However, I now understood that though my heart had been broken, I was finally beginning to come to terms with my own diagnosis.

I would have to rebuild my life from scratch, but this time I was going to build on all that I had learned along the way, drawing from experiences which had all helped me understand the things that I truly wanted out of life.

I was who I was because of my journey. I was the result of everything I had been through, both good and bad.

I now knew that all of these things have helped make me into who I am today.

NEW BEGINNINGS

I had been backed into a corner. I was left feeling like there was nowhere left to go, that my career was over, and that I now had no cards left to play. I realised I could either continue to exist as I had been, furthering the downwards spiral I was now being dragged into, or I would have to change the path I was on. I might not have had any cards left to play, but no-one of any importance knew that. It was time to resort to old habits: I knew that I was a hard worker and always did a good job, so I decided to trust that my reputation would precede me and that fate would, at some point, scoop me up.

It was this recent series of events that actually went on to inspire me to write this book. I had spent most of my life up to this point feeling worthless, thinking that what I had to give was unequal when compared to anything anyone else could offer. I had lived my life feeling inadequate, frightened, and ashamed to say what I really thought in case it was stupid or silly. Perhaps it was time to emerge from my self-imposed shadow and from behind my smile and shout from the rooftops, or from the pages of a book…

I am dyslexic.

I find things hard.

I battle everyday with myself and my brain, but I

never give up.

I don't let dyslexia stop me.

It was time to stop fighting it and to just let go. I had battled with myself throughout my entire life to keep my difficulties hidden. Every morning I had checked my armour was intact and prepared my weapon for the day: my smile. These two things had always protected me and kept me safe, but it was now time to just go with it. Just as the once hot rays of summer sun eventually dampen and render the trees with a golden, autumnal hue, I too now had to trust that I was on a natural journey with its own destination.

Why did I choose this metaphor in particular? Because just as the bare trees ride out the harsh winter, inevitably, April showers and spring airs encourage new shoots and leaves, all eager to once more soak up the warm rays from the sun. You can't fight nature, and I couldn't fight being dyslexic any longer. My battle to keep it hidden did not allow me to acknowledge my strengths: my instincts, my passion, my love for life and people, and my ability to think outside the box. Fighting dyslexia hadn't allowed me to just be 'me'.

While every season has its own unique beauty, each too has its own flaws. The summer brings long days and blue skies, but the raging sun suffocates the ground and browns the grass. Autumn sees the changing colours of trees as the leaves prepare to fall, but the dampness of early morning turns even the most determined of leaves to mulch and does not preserve their beauty. Winter glistens amidst freezing temperatures, but has the power to stop life in its tracks, covering the ground with a thick blanket of snow, leaving birds no longer able to find food.

Spring then has the hardest job of all with so many new beginnings, brought about from nothing. It hopes seeds that have planted themselves will succeed in reaching precious sunlight, striving to grow bigger and stronger than before. However, one harsh frost at just the wrong time can destroy vulnerable, fragile plants leaving them broken and lifeless, only the most resilient will win the chance to taste the summer sun. One season rolls continually into another, leaving the last season to fade away into memory, all the time building on existing beauty in the best way that nature can.

It was now time for me to stop looking backwards, instead to focus on what lay before me. Everything had changed. Well, actually everything had not really changed.

I had changed.

I felt free to breathe in a way I had never let myself breathe before.

I suddenly realised that my future was now unwritten, and my new course was entirely in my hands. I was in control of it; I could go anywhere I liked and do anything I wanted. I had done it. After 36 years I was finally free.

I was me.

No more, and no less.

I am good enough. I am equal. I am important, and no-one will ever make me feel any different. I would start a revolution on my own, refusing to return to a life of stress and unhappiness.

I would find another way, because there is always another way.

For the first time in my life I had no idea where I was going or where life was going to take me, however, I found it ironic that I felt less scared than I had been following the old safe and steady path that seemed mapped out for me!

Sometimes you need to take a leap of faith, trust, let go, and see what happens. I have taken that leap and those who matter have leapt with me. The people who matter watch on, smiling at me, and their smiles tell me that I am going to be ok. I am not relying on anyone catching me, instead I'll now catch myself when the time is right, and I will be in control.

I am going to use my strengths to define me. They will define my future…

EPILOGUE: THE BOY WHO WILL SUCCEED

Success:

"To achieve what you set out to do."

(Jo Rees, 2017)

My son continued to struggle at school. Despite still taking in everything verbally and, while he could sit and comfortably discuss a topic demonstrating a firm comprehension, the moment a pen was placed in his hand the wall went back up, and his ability to learn seemed to just fade away.

He wrote so slowly, often failing to finish anything he was writing, but more concerning was that he had now started to define himself by the things he couldn't do, constantly telling me how rubbish he was at everything. He had begun to lose interest in the world. This was not his school's fault, they were doing all they could to help him, no longer allowing him to hide his writing issues anymore. He was back in the main classroom, and they worked hard with him. While he was making progress, his self-esteem and confidence continued to dip and fade away.

He needed to begin to understand his own difficulties, and in doing so, begin to develop his own strategies to help himself, although by now he was no longer willing to take this help from me: his own mum. I had tried to help, showing him little tips and tricks I'd learnt both personally and professionally that might help him to understand and move forward, but he just wasn't listening to me.

Initially I felt this made me a failure, but I quickly realised that this wasn't about me and how I felt; this was about him, and what he needed. He was gifted at music, so I knew he would be able to learn an instrument. This was something I could arrange for him. I knew that this would not only make him feel good about himself, but this would also make him realise he was worth something! He started to learn the trumpet, which soon turned out to be something he was naturally good at, passing grades 1 and 2 with distinction.

While he was motivated, and had a naturally good ear for music, behind the scenes I knew how hard he was having to work to follow the music and the instructions, to remember the notes and rhythms, all the while knowing how easily his little brain could become overloaded. I knew from experience that his personal defence mechanism was to simply say 'I just won't do it anymore,' or 'I'll give up;' I'd lost count of how many times I had had these very same thoughts.

Unfortunately for my son, he has me as his mother, and I am an expert at playing his game. I know the loopholes, having played this game for thirty-six years myself. I know where to look, and I know where I can find him. I know he needs to get out from behind his barrier, and his own weapon of choice is disengagement. However, I can see through it, and I will not let him use it as a weapon against himself. He will be better equipped than my dad and I, because I know what needs to be done, and while I can't do it myself, I know where we can get help.

I drafted in a former manager of mine, herself once a specialist teacher of dyslexia, but now retired. I explained my concerns and she helped me. Well, actually, she helped him. She saw him once a week, helping him to build his confidence, she made him feel important, and she did not let him hide. Most importantly she taught him how to stay afloat and how to be visible in a classroom, where it is easy to hide.

Now aged 10, he knew what he needed to survive in a learning environment, and he knew he needed to verbalise his thoughts. He knew he needed to wear ear defenders when he wanted to think and get his head down, to block out the noise and language he did not need to process. He knew that he could use a spellchecker, knew how to look for key words in text, knew how he needed to sit near the front, knew how he needed to face the board and knew that he could ask for help. He knew he was able to tell his teacher what he needed. I think he probably drove them mad, but he was now in control. At ten years old, he was already secure in what he needed, and was well on his way to being successful.

Part of the reason why the tuition had such an impact was the relationship he had with his tutor was simply amazing. She knew exactly how far she could push him without him tipping into panic, but also knew when to pull him out from where he was hiding. Simply put, she could play his game better than him. I often dragged him into school, but he skipped away into tuition. There was something about the relationship that spurred him on. I suspect she smiled at him lots, constantly making him feel like he was making massive progress, even if the steps were, in fact, very small.

I'd say that the future looks bright for my son. While we still have a long way to go and we have to constantly keep on top of his self-esteem and confidence, he will get there although it may be a lifelong balancing act.

He won't need to hide because he will know what he needs to do to be successful. Not because I will be doing it for him, but because I will help him by teaching him the skills he needs, and finding the right people and resources to support him. Knowledge is power, and if we know that each of us has it within us to be an unstoppable force, then each of us has the ability to change the world…

As for me, I am changing the world. One step at a time!

As you know, I have written a book! It was two years in the making, and I did it thanks to that manager who employed me as a specialist teacher supporting dyslexia, and who went on to support my son. She believed in me, and I got there!

In that same two years, rather a lot has changed. After resigning from my job, I went on to become an intervention teacher at another primary school. As the autumn leaves fell once again and the evenings grew darker, a small flicker of light turned back into a flame. As an intervention teacher, I had been privileged enough to work with, and meet some rather brilliant children who reminded me not only why I had chosen teaching as my profession, but also of the difference that you can make. Despite going to work in the dark in the morning and driving back home in the dark each evening, without realising it those children helped me learn even more about myself that had, as yet, lay undiscovered.

They inspired me to be brave enough to set up my own company. In the cold winter month of January 2016, **Another Way Round** was born.

Another Way Round aims to raise the profile of dyslexia, making a positive difference to people by assessing, tutoring, empowering, and training people to not only know what to look for, but also the best ways to support dyslexia. It was difficult to decide what to call the company, but it was Unbiological who finally came up with the name, since I apparently constantly look for 'Another Way Round' and rarely give up!

That's also what I do with the pupils I work with; we keep going, trying different approaches until we find the strategy that works for them as an individual. **Another Way Round** has gone from strength to strength, and continues to grow and evolve with each passing day. As a company, we have has already worked with over two hundred people. I miss having colleagues, but setting up and running my own company has been the challenge I needed to reignite my passion for teaching and learning, seeing me continue my own training, undertaking further courses, and constantly driving me to extend my knowledge.

While there was no snow for us in the winter of 2016, the trees still fell bare and the roads were still icy. I knew, because I was now running on them! Never one to stand still, I had challenged myself to do something not only had I had never done before, but had never felt any desire to do. Against most of my family's better judgement, I registered to run a marathon.

I ran four times a week, and honestly had never felt better. Running makes me feel free. I often ran the same routes at the same time, and would bump into old ladies or men walking their dogs who would smile and wave, and strangers who would say 'Keep going' and smile at me. I would smile at them in return.

I completed the Brighton Marathon in April 2016, and in doing so raised £3000 for the charity PLANETS (Pancreatic, Liver and NeuroEndocrine TumourS) who have provided, and continue to provide, ongoing support to my uncle. That year also marked the twenty-year anniversary of my father-in-law's death, who died of pancreatic cancer in 1996.

It's true what they say, that it's only when you push yourself out of your comfort zone that you 'find yourself'. I'd felt invisible for so long, but when I ran I felt alive.

One of the main reasons I crossed the finishing line of the marathon was because my wonderful family were placed at strategic points across the 26.2 miles. My mum, dad, sister, uncles, aunt and cousins were, and continue to be with me every step of the way. I made it through because pretty much every message I received on the morning of the marathon, including messages from Nomad, KB, Fellow Smiler, Work Mum, and Always There. They all told me they believed I could do it, and I would not let them down!

Another Way Round supported lots of families and pupils through its first summer, with a number of workshops and free parent information sessions. We went on a mission to raise the profile of 'dyslexia and its hidden difficulties', with the organisation of a family fun event in June at a local water-sports business being a memorable highlight. We chose the summer's only day of torrential rain, but a little downpour did not deter us, and seventeen pupils managed to get out in a kayak and have the time of their lives. To this day, many of them still rave about the day they kayaked in the rain, but also because they did something new. Meanwhile, word of our work spread and the reputation of the company grew, and I began to be invited in by local schools to deliver training. There was not much time to look back on the journey that had brought me here because I was just too busy!

The summer was lush, with Scenic Route coming to stay, together with her gorgeous new-born son. We drank gin; we paddled in waves and got sand between our toes. She watched me sing, we ate ice cream, and for the first time ever I cried when she left. Tears of happiness, appreciating what her friendship meant to me.

The nights began to draw in, but still I demanded to swim in the sea until such time as it was dark with new allies known as the 'Healers'. Meanwhile, my son prepared for the transition to secondary school, this would stand as the only time since his illness shortly after his birth when I would feel genuinely scared as to what might become of him.

Amazingly, he took it all in his stride, and is surviving. In fact, he's doing more than just surviving, he is thriving!

The mornings were turning damp and dark and the warmth now falling out of the sun. In late September, The Trumpet Player turned 40, for which we threw him a party. It was a team effort, to which our nearest and dearest attended, including Five Minutes Fast. Mr. Unbiological settled the debt from years earlier for those 120 individually crafted Lego-brick cupcakes! He made shepherd pies to die for, feeding some thirty-four guests, carving The Trumpet Player's initials into the potato topping! It's these perfectionist's finishing touches that connect us dyslexics; the need to go the extra mile and, in doing so, create something unique.

I had started utilising social media to develop my knowledge and build a professional network. While I continued to seek out a publisher for my book, I had started writing my own blog. Posts from this had now made it as far away as Australia and America, and one post even resulted in me being interviewed via Skype from Australia! I continued to push myself out of my comfort zone, and in doing so made some wonderful connections!

My newly-forged links with the Helen Arkell Centre opened further doors for me, commissioning me to be involved in delivery of training as part of the National Neuro Diversity Project, funded by the DfE. I knew that they could not only see me as being 'me', but saw the potential in me immediately.

The training sessions I delivered were sandwiched around another unforeseen, and fairly significant event in my life. The first training in mid-October fell on my birthday; the second session took place on a cold, but bright, November day, just three weeks after my nan had passed away. It served as a cold reminder that not only are we immortal, but that we have to make every minute count.

As winter set back in again, my only work colleague, Albert the Tortoise, was now getting ready for his hibernation. I, on the other hand, felt stronger and more focused than ever. The stark days that followed were warmed by the glow of the company that I was nurturing and growing, each day moving surely in the direction that I was steering it in. On an almost-daily basis, this same journey presented me with amazing opportunities that I had only once dreamed of!

Time presses on, and spring is in the air again here; life still goes on, and the days just seem to tumble by me. Sometimes it still feels hard to breathe, but above all there is a new-found freedom in the positive differences I now seem to be making. Differences not only in my life, but in those of others.

On reflection, I don't think I would change any part of my story, my journey made me who I am.

For someone who can't really spell, and who never got an 'A' in her exams. For someone who generally forgets the things she needs to remember most, misplacing keys and other valuables all the time. For someone who is unable to proofread her own reports, and to this day doesn't know her multiplication tables by heart.

In spite of all these, and other things, I think I've done alright.

After all, remember…

"To be defined is not to dwell on what you cannot do, but to expose, polish, and shine the things you choose to do.

Only when you have exposed, polished, and shined your strengths are you able to be all that you are meant to be.

This is my definition, and this is my expectation of you."

(Jo Rees, 2015)

DISLEXIA RULES
ALWAYS THERE 120 CUPCAKES SUPERSTAR
UNDERRATED
SOLID AND RELIABLE HEALERS
FAMILY UNBIOLOGICALS
NOMAD
SCENIC ROUTE
WORKMUM
FELLOW SMILER
5 MINUETS FAST

DYSLEXIA THROUGH THE EYES OF OTHERS

Dyslexia displays and manifests itself in many different ways, and will affect everyone slightly differently owing to their own experiences, their personality, and their strengths. No two profiles are ever exactly the same.

'Don't Forget to Smile' discusses in detail about how dyslexia affected me, my son, my godson, and some of the children I have taught. To give you a wider view, I asked some of the children and adults I have worked with to tell me how dyslexia affects them. Here are some of their responses:

"Feeling frustrated when I can't understand things straight away, this makes me feel angry and cross with myself inside and cross with my teachers. It also makes me feel bad about myself."

"Feel different from everyone else at school... don't feel equal to them."

"Constantly having to read things over and over again but still not understanding it."

"Feeling insecure about spelling - which makes me have to use longer sentences in order to avoid attempting to spell the tricky word."

"Using a dictionary is really hard because I don't know the order of the alphabet, but sometimes also what letter I am looking for! "

"It's hard being corrected all the time, constantly worrying about whether what I am saying is right or not."

"Embarrassed at what others might think of me and not being as fast or even able to do what my friends can do in class."

"Writing feels such hard work and never being able to get the words I have in my head onto the paper because I can't organize them or spell the words I want."

"It takes ages for me to organize my ideas on paper"

"Looking blankly at someone who's just explained something but not in a way I understood!"

"I wish my teachers knew how hard I try to get my ideas on the paper and what hard work this is for me "

"Feeling terrified at being asked to read out loud at school."

"In jobs I have done the paperwork always gets in the way and makes it far more challenging for me than it needs to be."

"Not being able to copy from the board and constantly losing my place looking between the board and the page."

"The panic when tests are timed that I won't be able to do it. It makes me feel sick and my brain stops working making it seem even more difficult."

"Feeling stupid that I couldn't get the hang of shorthand, it felt like it was a code I could not crack."

"People not understanding that dyslexia has so many aspects to it."

"Never being given enough time! So never being able to complete work, the frustration this causes and also feeling of not wanting to bother if you know you won't complete it in the time."

"So often things seeming more complicated than they are!"

"Remembering things, like everyday things! PE kits and homework…"

"When reading books with lots of text it's hard to keep my place and I have a difficulty finding the next line."

"Sometimes when I read, I replace the word I am reading with another word that starts with the same two letters but is nothing like the original so confuses the sense the sentence so I have to reread it!"

"Never feeling confident on the inside or 100% like I know what I am doing."

"Feeling depressed, mostly from knowing I have a good brain and will never get to use it."

GLOSSARY OF ABBREVIATED TERMS

C-Section	Caesarean Section
DfE	Department for Education
DILP	Dyslexia Institute Literacy Programme
GP	General Practitioner [family doctor]
NQT	Newly Qualified Teacher
PGCE	Postgraduate Certificate of Education
SEN	Special Educational Needs
SENCo	Special Educational Needs Coordinator
SEND	Special Educational Needs and Disability
TA	Teaching Assistant

Printed in Great Britain
by Amazon

19549573R00140